Global Sport Leadership

This book explores the global developments in sport leadership and practice.

Drawing on the vast and ever-growing leadership literature, the book examines advances in leadership theory and practice in the context of the challenges faced by those working in global sport management positions. It explores the various dimensions of leadership, with a particular focus on the development of leadership theory. It also looks at the operational and contextual elements of leadership in a global sport environment and finally reflects on the status quo, and explores future challenges and research opportunities for leadership and global sport management.

Stephen Frawley is a Research Director at the Centre for Business and Social Innovation (CBSI), located at the University of Technology Sydney. Prior to joining academia, Stephen worked in the Sport Division for the Sydney 2000 Olympic and Paralympic Games Organising Committee (SOCOG).

Laura Misener is an Associate Professor and Acting Director at the School of Kinesiology, Faculty of Health Science, at Western University, Canada. Her research interests include the social impact of sport and events; disability sport and the Paralympic Games; physical activity and sport policy analysis; and the intersections of sport, physical activity, and health promotion.

Daniel Lock is a Principal Academic and the Head of Research and Professional Practice in the Department of Sport and Physical Activity at Bournemouth University; an Adjunct Associate Professor in Sport Management at Griffith University, Australia; and an Associate Editor of *Sport Management Review*.

Nico Schulenkorf is an Associate Professor of Sport Management at University of Technology Sydney. His research focusses on the social, cultural, and health-related outcomes of sport and event projects within and between disadvantaged communities.

Routledge Research in Sport Business and Management

For more information about this series, please visit https://www.routledge.com/
Routledge-Research-in-Sport-Business-and-Management/book-series/RRSBM

Global Sport Leadership

**Stephen Frawley, Laura Misener,
Daniel Lock and Nico Schulenkorf**

Routledge
Taylor & Francis Group

LONDON AND NEW YORK

First published 2019
by Routledge
2 Park Square, Milton Park, Abingdon, Oxon OX14 4RN

and by Routledge
52 Vanderbilt Avenue, New York, NY 10017

First issued in paperback 2020

Routledge is an imprint of the Taylor & Francis Group, an informa business

British Library Cataloguing-in-Publication Data
A catalogue record for this book is available from the British Library

Library of Congress Cataloging-in-Publication Data
Names: Frawley, Stephen, 1969– author. | Misener, Laura, author. | Lock, Daniel, author. | Schulenkorf, Nico, author.
Title: Global sport leadership / by Stephen Frawley, Laura Misener, Daniel Lock and Nico Schulenkorf.
Description: Abingdon, Oxon ; New York, NY : Routledge, 2019. | Series: Routledge research in sport business and management | Includes bibliographical references and index.
Identifiers: LCCN 2018059301
Subjects: LCSH: Sports administration. | Leadership. | Sports and globalization.
Classification: LCC GV716 .F73 2019 | DDC 796.06/9—dc23
LC record available at https://lccn.loc.gov/2018059301

ISBN 13: 978-0-367-67127-3 (pbk)
ISBN 13: 978-1-138-10531-7 (hbk)

Typeset in Galliard
by codeMantra

Contents

List of tables

1 Global sport leadership

Setting the scene

Introduction

Sport plays an important role in the lives of millions of people around the world. Whether it be watching the Olympic Games or the Football World Cup every four years, or participating in a weekly ParkRun event, sport impacts society socially, economically, and environmentally. Given the scope of this impact and the services needed to ensure each sport, and the associated competitions, can take place week after week and year after year, having people with the right leadership skills is crucial: whether that includes highly paid CEOs of professional leagues or volunteers delivering sport programmes in disadvantaged communities. Sport is both business and emotion, and it is imperative that leaders working in sport understand this unique feature. As such, leadership of sport is not solely important in the domain of elite sport. In fact, leadership is equally relevant to encouraging sport participation (in all its forms) in order for participants to realise the associated health and social benefits.

As the sport economy has grown dramatically across the globe over the past 40 years, so has the number of universities and colleges offering sport management and sport business education to train future managers and leaders. In addition to offering sport-specific subjects such as sport marketing, sport development, sport event management, sport media, and sport governance, many tertiary institutions offer sport-specific leadership subjects and programmes designed to provide students with the skills to lead in a fast changing business and political environment.

Global Sport Leadership was conceived with the express intent to engage sport management students and scholars with current, critical, and applied sport leadership knowledge. To achieve this aim, the book explores some key leadership issues that are faced by sport managers today, including implementing leadership development, leading in high performance sport environments, leading in sport for development environments, and understanding failed leadership. In the book, we address these issues from a critical management perspective. Specifically, we believe that sport, overall, can play a positive role in society; however, it also has a long history of corruption and ethically challenged management.

The book is structured in ten chapters. In this introductory chapter, we outline the purpose of the book and provide an overview of each chapter. We discuss how leadership as a concept has been defined and briefly explore the different approaches to understanding leadership that have emerged in the research literature in recent years. We also discuss the emergence of the sport/business leadership domain and possibilities for future leadership research.

In Chapter 2, we articulate the social identity approach to sport leadership in relation to three main objectives. First, we seek to provide an insight into *why* understanding groups is of fundamental importance to sound leadership. Second, we explain how valued social identities provide a basis for shared understandings of group values, mission, and visions toward which group members are energised to contribute. Third, we discuss how, through embodying prototypical (ideal) representations of a group, leaders can achieve power (and success) through the collective strengths of a group or organisation.

In Chapter 3, leadership development and succession management in the context of professional sport organisations are examined. In this chapter, the concept of leadership development is introduced, exploring the research that has been undertaken from both sport and non-sport perspectives. The work on experience-based leadership by McCall (2010) is cited as a useful framework to be applied by professional sport organisations in order to maximise leadership and management potential across all workforce levels. Finally, the importance of leadership development for professional sport organisations in the context of succession management is explored in detail.

In Chapter 4, the concept of cross-border leadership is introduced, and we propose a new and inclusive working definition. The specific traits and competencies of cross-border leaders are debated in the chapter. In addition, a discussion takes place on the specific challenges and future opportunities of cross-border leadership. Finally, the chapter illustrates how cross-border leadership can be applied in a sport context through a case study of the Pacific Islands nation of Fiji.

In Chapter 5, the role of leadership in the context of sport mega-events is examined in detail. The chapter explores two levels of mega-event leadership: (1) the urban development perspective on delivering civic outcomes and (2) the organising committee agenda when attempting to deliver a successful event. The analysis of these two levels draws upon multiple theoretical approaches, including work that is focussed on theories of event management and event legacy perspectives.

In Chapter 6, we explore leadership practices that support diversity and inclusion across the spectrum of sport delivery. The chapter outlines why the sport literature has been lacking with regard to understanding leadership from a diversity and inclusion perspective. A number of theoretical approaches that might support the creation of more socially just and diverse sport organisations are debated.

In Chapter 7, the leadership-specific aspects of sport for development are outlined and discussed. The chapter examines the most relevant leadership theory for this space and how it connects with recent sport for development research.

In order to demonstrate practical implications, a detailed case study is presented that explores the leadership challenges for sport organisations in the Pacific Island nation of Samoa.

In Chapter 8, we investigate leadership in the context of high performance sport. The chapter starts by outlining what actually constitutes high performance sport. It then discusses high performance sport policy and leadership at the various levels of elite sport. The role of both coaches and athletes as leaders is explored as are the relevant factors that shape and influence success.

In Chapter 9, with the assistance of Tessa McLachlan, we explore the concept of failed leadership. While it is the hope of every leader and organisation to provide positive and successful leadership, the reality is that often things go amiss, leaders fail, and individuals and stakeholders are impacted negatively. This chapter therefore explores the consequences for professional sport organisations of failed leadership, using one of the biggest-ever scandals to impact Australian sport: an event referred to as #Sandpapergate. In Chapter 10, the final chapter, we discuss the future opportunities and possibilities for sport leadership research and practice.

Defining leadership

While the concept of leadership is one of the most researched areas in the field of management studies, it has been viewed from both wide and narrow standpoints. Due to this confusion about how leadership should be viewed, multiple definitions have come to light over the past half-century (Egan, Sarros, & Santora, 1995). Given this it has been suggested that rather than trying to find the perfect single definition, leadership scholars should accept the value of diversity and encourage various definitions (Yukl, 1989). One way of doing so is presenting leadership as three interconnected levels: meta, macro, and micro (Frawley, Favaloro, & Schulenkorf, 2018; Nicholls 1987). The 'meta' level of leadership can be described as people exerting influence by creating a vision that attracts engaged followers (e.g. Google). The 'macro' level of leadership refers to executives building successful organisations via the creation of strong identities and culture. The 'micro' level relates to the performance of particular actions that require different responses depending on the situation. According to Nicholls (1987), when we examine leadership from this three-level perspective it is focussed on top-down and bottom-up approaches, demonstrating that leadership success is a dynamic construct.

Another point of confusion in the leadership literature is the distinction that is often made between leaders and managers. Soucie (1994) argues that leadership and management are interdependent concepts that, while overlapping, also have definitional differences. Similarly, Kotter (1990) has stated that managing is about seeking stability and order, while leading is about being adaptive and constructive to change. Another more common view is that management is doing things right, while leadership is doing the right things (Yukl, 1989). From this viewpoint, leading can be both formal and informal in nature, wh managing is more performance-related and takes into account formal managerial positioning. Leadership action therefore enables groups of people to work together in positive and meaningful ways, while management processes are more institutionally specific, i.e. less focussed on people and more focussed on specific tasks and activities (Day, 2000).

Over the recent history of leadership scholarship, a number of different perspectives have emerged that should be noted and briefly overviewed as background for the remaining chapters in the book. While not exhaustive, some of the foundational approaches to leadership studies include the following: situational leadership, authentic leadership, ethical leadership, transformational leadership, charismatic leadership, responsible leadership, and relational leadership. Each of these theoretical perspectives is explored in the following.

Situational leadership

Situational leadership can be described as the "interplay between the leader's guidance, direction and socio-emotional support, and the readiness ... that followers exhibit on a particular task" (Avery & Ryan, 2002, p. 243). Larsson and Vinberg (2010) also suggest that situational leadership can be explored via three elements: change orientation, structure orientation, and relation orientation. From this approach relation orientation is regarded as the foundation of successful leadership, while change orientation and structure orientation leadership are adopted differently depending on the specific situation.

Authentic leadership

According to Avolio and Gardner (2005) authentic leadership is considered "as all forms of positive leadership and its development" (p. 316). Authentic leadership is therefore considered as a continual learning process where leaders and followers attempt to gain self-awareness through open and trusting relationships. Avolio and Gardner (2005) further argue that authentic leadership can be generated through not only increasing one's self-awareness but also "self-regulation, and positive role modelling" (p. 317).

hical leadership

over a decade ago, Brown and Trevino (2006) suggested that the con-
thical leadership remained largely undeveloped. They stated that eth-
are "honest, caring and principled individuals who make fair and
ions", and establish clear ethical standards for all of their follow-
n the seemingly never-ending reporting of ethical scandals in
nd sport the value of the ethical dimension has never been
 all individuals and groups, including men and women,
another issue that needs ethical assessment. Business,
mains that to this day are still dominated by men in

senior leadership positions: to what extent in our modern world is this ethical? Issues of power, gender, and diversity provide both constraints to and possibilities for leaders forming relationships and delivering ethically to their institutions and communities (Sinclair, 2009).

Transactional and transformational leadership

Transformational leadership is possibly the most researched construct in the leadership literature (Parry, 1998). It is argued that this particular approach became popular partly due to the holistic perspective of the transactional-transformational leadership paradigm (Bass, 1997). This holistic paradigm is applied across various levels of leadership, including individual, group, organisational, and societal levels (Ryan, 2018). Bass (1999) also refers to these levels as micro, macro, and meta. According to Bass (1985, p. 26)

> the transformational leader is one who motivates followers to do more than they would normally be expected to do. As a result, the followers' original levels of confidence in reaching desired and designated outcomes as a result of performance are transformed.

While transformational leadership considers the group, we argue in Chapter 2 that social identity theorising of leadership has moved beyond transformational and transactional approaches because it provides a framework that explains how effective leadership results from creating groups that are meaningful to leaders and followers alike. As outlined by a recent study deploying social identity theory conducted by Smith, Haslam, and Neilsen (2018), leadership emerges "through interactions, processes and practices" that are perceived by members of a group or organisation "to develop and advance shared goals and shared identity" (p. 1425).

Charismatic leadership

Charismatic leadership is closely connected to transformational leadership (Conger, 1999). Charismatic leaders are said to "inspire in their followers unquestioning loyalty and devotion without regard for the followers' own self-interest" (Parry, 1994, p. 85). The idea of transformational leadership was developed as a way of overcoming the negative connotations often associated with the term charisma (Bass, 1999; Shamir et al., 2018). Scholars such as House and Howell (1992) and Conger (1999), however, argue that charisma is an all-inclusive term encapsulating inspiration, intellectual stimulation, and individualised consideration. More recently, interesting work on charismatic leadership has explored the moderating factors that occur at a societal level and the value erosion of followers (Gebert, Heinitz, & Buengeler, 2016). This work in particular has implications for the leaders of large sport organisations such as the International Olympic Committee.

Responsible leadership

The concept of responsible leadership has developed significant momentum over the past decade, with a number of studies completed within the broader area of management studies (Doh & Stumpf, 2005; Miska, Stahl, & Mendenhall, 2013; Pless, Maak, & Waldman, 2011; Stahl, Pless, & Maak, 2013; Voegtlin, Patzer, & Scherer, 2012; Waldman & Siegel, 2008). Responsible leadership offers the potential to combine work on leadership and corporate social responsibility (CSR) while also informing the sport management literature. Defining what is responsible leadership, though, has not been without its challenges, especially given its similarities to ethical leadership. Waldman and Siegel (2008) have suggested that responsible leadership must involve all key stakeholders in decision-making in order to ensure the sustainability of the relevant organisation. Other researchers have argued that to be a truly responsible leader, those in positions of power must ensure that they have a positive influence across the three key areas in the triple bottom line (i.e. economic impact, environmental impact, and social impact; Savitz & Weber, 2006). Others have proposed that responsible leaders first 'do good' and second 'do no harm', i.e. they do not make matters any worse than they already are (Brown & Trevino, 2006). Overall, Stahl et al. (2013) suggest that responsible leaders should act both for the local and for the global, mastering leadership challenges around the domains of sustainability, ethics, diversity, and citizenship.

Relational leadership

According to Cunliffe and Eriksen (2011), relational leadership "requires a way of engaging with the world in which the leader holds herself/himself as always in relation with, and therefore morally accountable to others" (p. 1425). Furthermore, this approach "recognizes the inherently polyphonic and heteroglossic nature of life; and engages in relational dialogue" (p. 1425). Relational leadership has become one of the more frequently utilised approaches to leadership theory in recent times, particularly for those who come from a critical management theoretical perspective (Stephens & Carmeli, 2017). Relational leadership has practical implications in assisting leaders in understanding how important day-to-day relationships are and consequently how the everyday and mundane conversations and dialogue impact how we all lead.

Sport/Business leadership domain

As outlined, the generic leadership body of knowledge has grown substantially over the past half-century. However, while sport has been viewed as a worthy environment in which to conduct management research (Weese & Nicholls, 1987; Wolfe et al., 2005), leadership studies deploying sport have been relatively infrequent (Fletcher & Wagstaff, 2009; Fletcher & Arnold, 2011). Given the dramatic commercial growth of sport across the world over the past 50 years, and the resulting pressures and impacts that have emerged for leaders within the sport industry, it is curious that academic research has barely explored the key issues at hand. CEOs, presidents, coaches, sporting directors, and related senior sport management roles not only face relentless daily media scrutiny but also must perform to the very high standards expected by the general community and multiple stakeholders, including but not limited to sponsors, government, athletes, and fans (Ferkins & Shilbury, 2012; Hoye & Doherty, 2011). The investigation of sport leadership is therefore a complex area of study but one that provides an opportunity for different ways of thinking and knowledge development that benefits not only sport management but also the broader field of management studies (Chelladurai, 1980; Kellet, 1999; Marjoribanks & Farquharson, 2016).

Though progress has been slow, business and sport leadership research has started to cross the sport-business divide, acknowledging that there are valuable lessons to be learned from each other (Goff, 2005). Subsequently, a small body of research promoting the transfer of elite performance principles from the sport domain to the business domain has emerged (Burnes & O'Donnell, 2011; Goff, 2005; Jones, 2002; Kellet, 1999; Westerbeek & Smith, 2005). As outlined by Burnes and O'Donnell (2011):

> effective leadership is as crucial to success in sport as it is to business; There are areas where sports leaders are ahead of their business counterparts, particularly in developing the full potential of teams and individuals; [and], Sport offers a more holistic approach to leadership development, going beyond the business approach.
>
> (p. 17)

Furthermore, and as argued by Goff (2005), great leaders in sport need to be thinkers and not just "give-me-the-bottom-line" leaders (p. 222). They require mental strength and the ability to resolve interpersonal and management challenges quickly without being overwhelmed. Day et al. (2012) suggest, moreover, that while the non-sport domain of business can learn a great deal from their counterparts in sport, sport also has a considerable amount to learn from excellence in business. While first steps have been made to transfer knowledge across these domains, the literature base on sport leadership remains a developing field of study that requires greater investigation and research to further our understanding (Day, Gordon, & Fink, 2012). With this book, we aim to contribute to bringing the fields closer together and providing innovative perspectives on critical areas of global sport leadership.

In summary, *Global Sport Leadership* aims to address some of the aforementioned gaps in the literature and contribute new perspectives and approaches to studying sport leadership. We start this in Chapter 2 by examining the growing place of social identity theory in the leadership literature and how it can be applied to sport.

References

Avery, G. C., & Ryan, J. (2002). Applying situational leadership in Australia. *Journal of Management Development, 21*(4), 242–262.

Avolio, B. J., & Gardner, W. L. (2005). Authentic leadership development: Getting to the root of positive forms of leadership. *The Leadership Quarterly, 16*(3), 315–338.

Bass, B. M. (1985). Leadership: Good, better, best. *Organizational Dynamics, 13*(3), 26–40.

Bass, B. M. (1997). Does the transactional–transformational leadership paradigm transcend organizational and national boundaries? *American Psychologist, 52*(2), 130.

Bass, B. M. (1999). Two decades of research and development in transformational leadership. *European Journal of Work and Organizational Psychology, 8*(1), 9–32.

Brown, M. E., & Treviño, L. K. (2006). Ethical leadership: A review and future directions. *The Leadership Quarterly, 17*(6), 595–616.

Burnes, B., & O'Donnell, H. (2011). What can business leaders learn from sport? *Sport, Business and Management: An International Journal, 1*(1), 12–27.

Chelladurai, P. (1980). Leadership in sports organizations. Canadian journal of applied sport sciences. *Canadian Journal of Applied Sport Sciences, 5*(4), 226–231.

Conger, J. A. (1999). Charismatic and transformational leadership in organizations: An insider's perspective on these developing streams of research. *The Leadership Quarterly, 10*(2), 145–179.

Cunliffe, A. L., & Eriksen, M. (2011). Relational leadership. *Human Relations, 64*(11), 1425–1449.

Day, D. V. (2000). Leadership development: A review in context. *The Leadership Quarterly, 11*(4), 581–613.

Day, D. V., Gordon, S., & Fink, C. (2012). The sporting life: Exploring organizations through the lens of sport. *The Academy of Management Annals, 6*(1), 397–433.

Doh, J. P., & Stumpf, S. A. (Eds.). (2005). *Handbook on responsible leadership and governance in global business.* Cheltenham: Edward Elgar Publishing.

Egan, R. F., Sarros, J. C., & Santora, J. C. (1995). Putting transactional and transformational leadership into practice. *Journal of Leadership Studies, 2*(3), 100–123.

Ferkins, L., & Shilbury, D. (2012). Good boards are strategic: What does that mean for sport governance? *Journal of Sport Management, 26*(1), 67–80.

Fletcher, D., & Arnold, R. (2011). A qualitative study of performance leadership and management in elite sport. *Journal of Applied Sport Psychology, 23*(2), 223–242.

Fletcher, D., & Wagstaff, C. R. (2009). Organizational psychology in elite sport: Its emergence, application and future. *Psychology of Sport and Exercise, 10*(4), 427–434.

Frawley, S., Favaloro, D., & Schulenkorf, N. (2018). Experience-based leadership development and professional sport organizations. *Journal of Sport Management, 32*(2), 123–134.

Gebert, D., Heinitz, K., & Buengeler, C. (2016). Leaders' charismatic leadership and followers' commitment—The moderating dynamics of value erosion at the societal level. *The Leadership Quarterly, 27*(1), 98–108.

Goff, B. L. (2005). *From the ballfield to the boardroom: Management lessons from sports.* Westport, CT: Greenwood Publishing Group.

House, R. J., & Howell, J. M. (1992). Personality and charismatic leadership. *The Leadership Quarterly, 3*(2), 81–108.

Hoye, R., & Doherty, A. (2011). Nonprofit sport board performance: A review and directions for future research. *Journal of Sport Management, 25*(3), 272–285.

Jones, G. (2002). Performance excellence: A personal perspective on the link between sport and business. *Journal of Applied Sport Psychology, 14*(4), 268–281.

Kellet, P. (1999). Organisational leadership: Lessons from professional coaches. *Sport Management Review, 2*(1), 150–171.

Kotter, J. P. (1990). *How leadership differs from management.* New York: Free Press, 240, 59–68.

Larsson, J., & Vinberg, S. (2010). Leadership behaviour in successful organisations: Universal or situation-dependent? *Total Quality Management, 21*(3), 317–334.

Marjoribanks, T., & Farquharson, K. (2016). Contesting competence: Chief executive officers and leadership in Australian Football League clubs. *Marketing Intelligence & Planning, 34*(2), 188–202.

McCall, M. W. (2010). Recasting leadership development. *Industrial Organisational Psychology, 3*(1), 3–19.

Miska, C., Stahl, G. K., & Mendenhall, M. E. (2013). Intercultural competencies as antecedents of responsible global leadership. *European Journal of International Management, 7*(5), 550–569.

Nicholls, J. (1987). Leadership and logic. *Management Decision, 25*(4), 28–32.

Parry, K. W. (1994). Transformational leadership: An Australian investigation of leadership behaviour. In A. Kouzmin, L. V. Still, & P. Clarke (Eds.), *New directions in management* (pp. 82–114). Sydney: McGraw.

Parry, K. W. (1998). The new leader: A synthesis of leadership research in Australia and New Zealand. *Leadership Studies, 5*(4), 82–105.

Pless, N. M., Maak, T., & Stahl, G. K. (2011). Developing responsible global leaders through international service-learning programs: The Ulysses experience. *Academy of Management Learning & Education, 10*(2), 237–260.

Ryan, P. (2018). *Leadership: Circles of trust.* Sydney: Corwin.

Savitz, A., & Weber, W. (2006). *The triple bottom line: How today's best-run companies are achieving economic, social and environmental success.* New York: Josseybass.

Shamir, B., Arthur, M. B., & House, R. J. (2018). The rhetoric of charismatic leadership: A theoretical extension, a case study, and implications for research. In I. Katz, G. Eilam-Shamir, R. Kark, Y. Berson (Eds.), *Leadership now: Reflections on the legacy of Boas Shamir* (pp. 31–49). Bingley: Emerald Publishing Limited.

Sinclair, A. (2009). Seducing leadership: Stories of leadership development. *Gender, Work and Organization, 16*(2), 266–284.

Smith, P., Haslam, S. A., & Nielsen, J. F. (2018). In search of identity leadership: An ethnographic study of emergent influence in an interorganizational R&D team. *Organization Studies, 39*(10), 1425–1447.

Soucie, D. (1994). Effective managerial leadership in sport organizations. *Journal of Sport Management, 8*(1), 1–13.

Stahl, G. K., Pless, N. M., & Maak, T. H. O. M. A. S. (2013). Responsible global leadership. In M. E. Mendenhall, J. Osland, A. Bird, G. R. Oddou, M. J. Stevens, M. Maznevski, & G. K. Stahl (Eds.), *Global leadership: Research, practice, and development* (pp. 240–259). London: Routledge.

Stephens, J. P., & Carmeli, A. (2017). 13. Relational leadership and creativity: The effects of respectful engagement and caring on meaningfulness and creative work involvement. In M. Mumford, S. Hemlin (Eds.), *Handbook of research on leadership and creativity* (pp. 273–296). Cheltenham, UK: Edward Elgar Publishing.

Voegtlin, C., Patzer, M., & Scherer, A. G. (2012). Responsible leadership in global business: A new approach to leadership and its multi-level outcomes. *Journal of Business Ethics, 105*(1), 1–16.

Waldman, D. A., & Siegel, D. (2008). Defining the socially responsible leader. *The Leadership Quarterly, 19*(1), 117–131.

Weese, J., & Nicholls, E. (1987). Team leadership: Selection and expectations. *Physical Educator, 44*(1), 269.

Westerbeek, H., & Smith, A. (2005). *Business leadership and the lessons from sport.* New York: Palgrave Macmillan.

Wolfe, R. A., Weick, K. E., Usher, J. M., Terborg, J. R., Poppo, L., Murrell, A. J., … Simmons Jourdan, J. (2005). Sport and organisational studies. *Journal of Management Inquiry, 14*(2), 182–210.

Yukl, G. (1989). Managerial leadership: A review of theory and research. *Journal of Management, 15*(2), 251–289.

2 A social identity approach to sport leadership

Introduction

The notion of leading implies an individual, or individuals, who are able to exert social influence over others (Turner, Reynolds, & Subasic, 2008). Influencing others, however, can be difficult for a couple of reasons. First, the organisations or groups a person seeks to influence might be fragmented, divided, or disenfranchised. In this scenario, a [potential] leader would encounter personal agendas, schisms, and subgroups that make creating a shared purpose more complex. Second, some effective leaders can become ineffective when undertaking leadership of another group (e.g. David Moyes's leadership of Manchester United). In both examples, group dynamics are central to any understanding of leadership success. Developing a set of understandings that group members share provides a foundation through which common purpose and vision may be cultivated (Haslam & Platow, 2007). From the perspective that groups are crucial to successful leadership, it is surprising that much leadership research to date tends to focus on either (1) the characteristics of great leaders (i.e., men) or (2) the capacity of leaders to energise individuals rather than groups (Haslam, Reicher, & Platow, 2011).

In the present chapter, we draw on the social identity approach to leadership (Haslam et al., 2011), which provides a framework that explores how collective understandings (i.e. 'we' and 'us') of groups influence leadership. Rather than assuming that a certain 'type' of person or 'personality profile' predisposes an individual to leadership, through understanding group dynamics in context, social identity theorists seek to understand (1) *what effective leadership is in specific situations* and, given the knowledge of (1), (2) *who* might be *an effective leader* for a group. In this sense, the identity *that leader[s] and their followers share* provides a frame of reference for the *style* and *individual* most suitable to offer effective leadership in a given group or context. To bring this point to life, we might ask a simple question: would Tim Paine (current Australian Cricket Captain) or Sharni Williams (Captain of Australian Women's Rugby team) have the 'right' traits or be the 'correct' person to lead the Sydney Symphony Orchestra? We would argue not, and the social identity approach provides a detailed framework to explain why this is the case. In order to articulate the social identity approach to leadership, in the following chapter we

1   Introduce the social identity approach to groups
2   Explain the relationship between social identity, context, and leadership
3   Discuss the influence of leader prototypicality on leadership success.

The social identity approach

To introduce the social identity approach (social identity theory and self-categorisation theory combined), we ask the reader to consider their favourite sporting team. Now, imagine the team has lost a match against a fierce rival in a key match (e.g. the Wallabies have lost to the All Blacks). In social identity theory, Tajfel and Turner (1979) argue that individuals define a part of their self in terms of the identities they share with other people (e.g. with a sporting team). At the heart of social identity theory, Tajfel and Turner focussed on processes of *intergroup* comparison that led to evaluations of in-group and out-group[s] status. In the previous example, a loss to the All Blacks creates a strong identity threat for Australian Rugby fans on two levels. First, loss of any kind threatens group status. Second, loss to a rival creates a double whammy effect because the status of a rival increases, while the status of the in-group [temporarily] decreases. Understanding such status dynamics is important because when a group we identify with suffers from a negative intergroup comparison (e.g. a loss to a rival) the connotations do not end with the group – they also reflect on our self-concept (Cialdini et al., 1976). As such, the social groups we identify are important expressions of who we are and how we fit into society.

To understand how individuals come to define their self-concept in terms of group membership[s], we need to explore how individual perception shifts from understandings of self (i.e. 'I' and 'me') to collective evaluations ('us' and 'we'; Turner, 1982). Turner and Brown (1978) argued that people define who they are in terms of personal (i.e. unique and differentiated) and social identity (i.e. in terms of shared group membership; Turner et al., 2008). In this chapter, we are interested in the implications of social identities for leadership, which are made possible through a process of self-categorisation. Turner (1985) explicitly drew a distinction between social and self-categories. The former, he asserted, are externally attributed to an individual (e.g. dumb or lazy) and, therefore, may have no bearing on how he or she defines him or herself. If a social category has no bearing on a person's self-definition, it will have minimal influence on thought or action (and, as a result, leadership). On the other hand, self-categories are actively chosen as desirable statements of self that emphasise 'our' values, interests, or goals (Haslam et al., 2011). Self-categories are important as they provide a social and psychological basis for people to share meaningful group identities.

Group identities activate in contexts that render them useful in making sense of social situations (Oakes, Turner, & Haslam, 1991). Therefore, the transition from personal to social identity is not a permanent transition but a social and cognitive response to shifts in social life. A shift in social context might involve members of the in-group meeting, exposure to members of an out-group, or other shifts in the environment that are relevant to the *content* of an identity (Reed, 2002). To understand this point, one might consider a female accountant. During work hours, she is a devoted member of her organisation who works towards fulfilling her responsibilities in relation to the organisational purpose. In this sense, she identifies with a meaningful self-category shared with other members of the organisation. However, when work finishes, she is a keen badminton player and volunteer soccer coach. Participation in each of these contexts activates different – meaningful – group identities (i.e. work, badminton, and soccer). Thus, while the work, badminton, and soccer identities are always a part of her self-concept, they are only *salient* in contexts that render them relevant (Lock & Heere, 2017).

When rendered salient, meaningful group identities imbue members with contextually specific values, beliefs, and behaviours that define the in-group in contrast to other groups (or rivals; Tajfel & Turner, 1979). This does not imply that individuals lose themselves when a group identity activates in their self-concept. Rather, it implies that individuals *choose* to follow in-group norms because they are meaningful expressions of self in social situations (Haslam et al., 2011). Such norms provide behavioural blueprints that contain fuzzy guides about how group members (we) behave, dress, and act. Of more relevance to the present chapter, norms also provide a frame of reference through which *we interpret the actions of other people*. Therefore, as norms provide members with an understanding of *how to behave*, they also provide a *framework* to evaluate the *actions of other group members*. Behaviours that conform to in-group norms (where group norms are clear and shared by members), are more likely to be interpreted positively (Haslam et al., 2011) and, in turn, provide a platform through which an actor may obtain social influence and power within the collective (Turner, 2005).

Behaviour in accordance with in-group norms provides individuals with a legitimate platform to influence other group members (Turner, 2005). From a social identity perspective, 'legitimate power' stands opposed to power over individuals, which infers an approach to leadership whereby resources or rewards are conditional on individual or group performance (i.e. transactional leadership). Power over individuals can never engender true support from followers because extrinsic rewards motivate members. In situations where influence and *power are achieved through the group*, members understand what makes the group distinctive and, because of these factors, *choose* to contribute to shared goals because they are meaningful (Haslam et al., 2011). Therefore, efforts to influence other group members or, more specifically, to exert power over other group members relate strongly to the extent that such efforts embody or exemplify the shared group identity.

To return to the example of David Moyes arriving at Manchester United Football Club, he faced a somewhat impossible challenge of replacing Sir

Alex Ferguson after 27 years of leadership, not just of the team – but of the club (Elberse, 2013). Arriving at the club with his own methods – which had proven successful at Everton Football Club but were different from Ferguson's approach – Moyes was sacked in April 2014 after a largely unsuccessful tenure less than 12 months into his leadership. His tenure at Manchester United – as did Ferguson's – provides critical insights into the social identity approach to leadership, which we discuss in the case study later in this chapter. To summarise this brief introduction to the relevant parts of the social identity approach:

1   The groups we belong to play an important role in how we define ourselves
2   Self-categorisation shifts our frame of reference from personal to social identity
3   Group identities activate in our self-concept to influence behaviour in context
4   Salient social identities lead to thought and behaviour that aligns with in-group norms
5   Norms provide a framework to evaluate social influence and power.

Social identity approach to leadership

A fundamental point to begin the social identity analysis of leadership is that some people gain "disproportionate influence, through possession of consensual prestige or the exercise of power, or both, over the attitudes, behaviours and destiny of group members" (Hogg, 2001, p. 188). The social identity approach explains *why* some individuals are able to develop unity amongst group members and social influence (Ellemers, De Gilder, & Haslam, 2004; Haslam & Platow, 2007). In order to achieve such unity, leaders have a fundamental need to establish a sense of 'we' and 'us' through an agenda and purpose which resonates with followers. Therefore, in the following section, we draw on the extensive theoretical framework advanced by Haslam et al. (2011) to explore the types and levels of groups that can be led, the importance of leaders representing the in-group *prototype*, and entrepreneurial strategies to cultivate and embed identity in groups.

Category boundaries and content

Our discussion of social identity leadership requires some clarification in relation to the types of leader and levels of group one might encounter. Initially, it is important to note that social identity theorists do not subscribe to a paradigm in which there are homogeneous characteristics of great leaders (Haslam et al., 2011). Instead, the characteristics of the group and its contextual circumstances provide the most informative content to make sense of 'ideal' leader characteristics from context to context. Moreover, we might supplant the term *leader* in a variety of contexts because the social and contextual characteristics might be conducive to leaders or leadership groups. In the following discussion, our focus remains on the person or persons who are able to gain social influence in certain situations *in order to lead* (Turner et al., 2008).

Individuals can identify with a repertoire of groups that shape thought and action. Furthermore, from our discussion of the social identity approach, it should also be clear that various group identities can activate in a person's self-concept to influence behaviour when they are relevant to the social context (see Point 3). For example, a woman's organisational and gender identity might activate simultaneously in circumstances surrounding equal pay. Therefore, as an initial step in any task that requires leadership, there is a need to consider group boundaries (i.e. where the group starts and finishes). Take, for example, Netball Australia, whose current CEO is Marne Fechner. The category boundaries she deals with concern the sport of Netball and *all of its departments* and *operations*. From the social identity perspective, Fechner is responsible for cultivating an identity that – in an ideal situation – *all* members of Netball Australia and its audiences *share* (e.g. marketers, human resources, players, and fans). Within this overarching (or more abstract identity) is the Australian Women's Netball team, currently coached by Lisa Alexander. On a day-to-day basis, Alexander leads a smaller group of Samsung Diamonds players, coaches, and staff for whom she – in collaboration with members of the leadership group (e.g. senior players and coaching staff) – is responsible for creating a unity of vision and purpose, leading to success on the court. For an example of the various groups and levels of operation in a professional organisation, see https://netball.com.au/about-netball-australia/netball-australia-staff/. In each Netball Australia example, the respective leaders need to understand the group of people from whom they are seeking to engender support (Haslam et al., 2011).

Defining category boundaries also gives leaders the opportunity to develop knowledge about what group members *already share*. Understanding what values, beliefs, norms, and behaviours currently exist within a group are crucial starting points to establish a leadership approach that is sensitive to the existing identity. Reicher, Spears, and Haslam (2010) argue that when new leaders seek to lead established groups, a major objective should be to *emulate* key facets of the shared identity. Rather than bowing to the consensus and disregarding their own perspective, emulation demonstrates to followers that a new leader acknowledges, understands, and values features of the existing identity. This approach recognises that group identities are social and historical constructs that require tacit understanding before a new leader can achieve evolution or change. Furthermore, without a nuanced understanding of the normative content of an identity, a new leader will struggle to achieve social influence, a point we discuss next.

In-group prototypicality

In the discussion of social influence and power in groups, we discussed how actions that were perceived to be in-group normative were – on balance – more likely to be interpreted favourably by other group members (Levine, Prosser,

Evans, & Reicher, 2005; Turner, 2005). This is because behaviours that align with in-group norms are perceived as contributing to the achievement of shared goals. Therefore, we might dismiss the importance of leader characteristics and personality. Yet there is consistent evidence that leaders possess certain qualities, a point which requires reconciliation in relation to the social identity perspective (see Platow & van Knippenberg, 2001). Previous literature reveals that there are stereotypical perceptions of the qualities possessed by all good leaders (e.g. charisma, character, and personality). However, all of these features of good leaders are perceived in social contexts. For example, a leader might be perceived as highly charismatic in one group because he exemplifies norms and standards shared by group members. Likewise, in a different group with a different set of shared understanding, he might suffer from perceptions that he lacks charisma. Platow and van Knippenberg (2001) and Haslam et al. (2011) provide a detailed analysis arguing that personality and charisma are construed subjectively in relation to context. As such, to understand the traits or personalities that might be well suited to leading in a given situation, leaders must understand the notion of *prototypicality*.

Leader prototypicality moves beyond notions of the stereotypical leader to consider how the social and contextual features of group life influence follower construal of leader actions. The notion of in-group prototypicality reflects the extent to which a person or an action embodies what is shared by group members in contrast to out-groups (Hogg, 2001; Hogg & Terry, 2000; Turner, Hogg, Oakes, Reicher, & Wetherell, 1987). A core proposition of social identity theorists is that the contextual environment is fundamentally related to the shared understandings of a group that are most relevant to a given context (i.e. the in-group prototype; Turner et al., 1987). For example, when the All Blacks play England one week and Australia the next, the in-group prototype will shift to reflect *what makes the All Blacks positively distinctive in relation to each nation*. As the social context of group membership and the salient out-group changes over time, the ideal embodiment of the group changes as well. It follows, then, that effective leaders – beyond stereotypic qualities – will act in a manner that exemplifies the group identity and, by consequence, the in-group's distinctive qualities in relation to other groups.

Team sports, in particular, present fascinating challenges in this regard. Within leagues, teams are required to cooperate and compete (Shilbury, Quick, Westerbeek, Funk, & Karg, 2014). Furthermore, in most instances, the out-groups that sports teams face – while some rivals will be more salient than others (Tyler & Cobbs, 2017) – also change from week to week. This has connotations for the in-group prototype and, as a consequence, the actions that will be deemed to embody the shared identity a leader seeks to lead (Haslam et al., 2011). In terms of on-field leaders, this might see more aggressive players become prototypical in challenging or physical games, or skilful ones becoming prototypical in games that require greater demands for creativity.

In the same way that behaving in accordance with in-group norms confers influence and power on members, individuals who exemplify the in-group prototype in social contexts are viewed as legitimate sources of authority. Underscoring why leader prototypicality is so important, Haslam et al. (2011) discuss how group members view prototypical leaders as trustworthy and authentic exemplars of an identity. Individuals that exemplify the in-group prototype have been shown to be more popular figures in groups (Hogg, van Knippenberg, & Rast, 2012). Furthermore, prototypical leaders are more likely to galvanise followers because of perceptions that they have "the best interests of the group at heart" (Giessner & van Knippenberg, 2008, p. 30). This heightened level of trust affords leaders what Giessner and van Knippenberg term a 'licence to fail' because through their actions – even when unsuccessful – prototypical leaders are often still viewed as acting in the best interests of the group. The question then becomes, how do prototypical leaders build, develop, and change shared group understandings?

Identity entrepreneurs

To this point, we have outlined how leaders that embody the in-group prototype are able to assume a position of social influence and power. This is a position that acknowledges that (1) leaders need to be responsive to contextual shifts in the social environment in order to align their actions with the in-group prototype, and (2) some contextual situations might render certain leaders more prototypical than others. Acknowledging these points, and that in-group prototypes are not static constructs but, rather, constantly evolving features of the social and contextual environment, Reicher and his colleagues have explored how leaders act as identity entrepreneurs (Reicher, Haslam, & Hopkins, 2005; Reicher & Hopkins, 1996). Instead of merely conforming to the in-group prototype, entrepreneurial leaders engage in a process of 'making and remaking' identities in a manner that includes as many category members as possible (Reicher & Hopkins, 1996). (Referring to the earlier discussion of category boundaries, this could be a team of six or a country of millions.) Skilful leaders remake identities in a manner that enables them to embody the emerging in-group prototype. As such, skilled leaders play a major role in shaping the content of the identity when they are able to generate buy-in from followers through the embodiment of a nuanced understanding of the (1) historical context and (2) values and aspirations shared by group members.

The historically and socially constructed totems, symbols, values, and norms that accumulate over time are important representations of groups that make them distinctive in relation to key out-groups. Take, for example, a new leader of Australian Cricket assuming their position and making the following decision. To engage a younger audience, the incoming leader decides to refresh the headwear worn by the Australian Test Team by discontinuing the 'Baggy Green' and installing a new 'Trucker Hat' instead (i.e. reminiscent of Big Bash 20/20 headwear). It is fair to assume that reactions to the removal of this iconic symbol of the Australian Test Cricket identity (the 'Baggy Green' has been worn by Bradman, Chappell[s], Miller, Thomson, Waugh[s], etc.) would be severe from ex-players, commentators, fans, and so on. In this regard, it would represent a leadership action that would strongly violate the in-group prototype. A more sensible option for an incoming leader of Cricket Australia might be to prioritise developing participation in 'Australia's Game' (broadening the inclusivity and appeal of the group to 'All Australians'); success in the Ashes (thus activating a key out-group for comparison in followers minds); and World Cup success in long and short one-day formats (again, including followers that are interested in either short-form of cricket). In the latter example, the new leader is emphasising the similarity of their own leadership agenda with prototypical features of the in-group, which is likely to earn him or her an initial platform to lead rather than immediately attacking a key symbol of the shared identity.

In this regard, leaders need to innovate around the existing norms, values, and beliefs to cultivate an identity that members will share and that will allow the leader to embody the in-group prototype (Haslam et al., 2011). Such innovations can arise from developing the in-group identity based around underused or forgotten features of organisational heritage as well as extensions of its historical context (Reicher et al., 2005). For efficacy, such shifts should place the leader as a key embodiment of the new values, beliefs, or actions in relation to defined out-groups. Rather than distinguishing the leader from the group, any innovation should seek to place the leader *as one of the group*. Then, through in-group prototypicality, the leader will have the scope to further the visions of the group by galvanising followers who derive meaning and significance from the achievement of collective goals (i.e. power through the group).

In attempts to garner support from in-group members and manage the identity in complex circumstances, some leaders might seek to actively manipulate the social context and its effect on the ideal representation of the in-group (Reicher & Hopkins, 1996). In situations where group status comparisons are negative due to repeated losses, the coach or manager (depending on the sport) are likely to suffer from a concomitant reduction in the extent to which they are perceived to embody the [ideal] in-group identity. This raises a major problem as it is crucial that leaders in such situations retain 'control' of the group (Elberse, 2013). One social tactic that leaders adopt in such an instance is changing the out-group being used for comparative purposes or shifting the dimension on which the comparison is made (e.g. from winning to fair play; Lalonde, 1992). Jose Mourinho has used this tactic repeatedly throughout his career where, instead of owning up to his own or team failings, he will verbally render another out-group salient (e.g. referees), or manipulate the dimension of comparison, to shift the in-group prototype. Rather than admitting that Manchester City (as of 2018) are superior, Mourinho activates perceptions of the rival's spending in the transfer market (despite Manchester United's frivolity in the same area) in contrast to their main geographical rival. In doing so, Mourinho is actively attempting to lead the identity, in context, from a negative comparison of performance with the league leaders (i.e. Manchester City leading the Premier League) to a positive comparison surrounding the authenticity of the club (e.g. Bate, 2018). This subtle shift in the frame of reference allows Mourinho to place Pep Guardiola as the 'inheritor' of a strong squad while diminishing his predecessor at Manchester United, Louis van Gaal, who 'left him with nothing' (Robson, 2018). That is, he set out to cultivate his prototypicality as a highly effective group leader, considering (1) the failures of previous leaders and (2) the frivolous spending of Manchester City as the salient out-group.

Although innovative leaders act as identity entrepreneurs, it is important to emphasise that the process is not unidirectional – at least it should not be. Reicher et al. (2005) describe the ideal process as being dialogic and the result of interactions between leaders and followers. The dialogic process gives followers an active voice in defining what 'we' do. In turn, such empowerment enhances the degree to which the resultant innovations will be congruent with the values and aspirations shared by participants. As we have discussed, such congruence is central to cultivating shared understandings of 'us' that are meaningful to group members.

Case study – Manchester United and Alex Ferguson

In order to apply the social identity approach further, we now revisit the example of Alex Ferguson's retirement and David Moyes's hiring at Manchester United. In her research exploring Alex Ferguson's success, Elberse (2013), explores what made the ex-Manchester United manager one of the greatest in history. Implicitly, this case study – and the hiring of David Moyes – provides excellent ground to which to apply the main features we have discussed in this chapter. Elberse (2013) describes how Ferguson set standards (norms) he expected all members of the group to exemplify. He embedded values such as hard work, commitment, and determination in the culture shared by members of the team and organisation.

Importantly, these were values that Ferguson famously exemplified, which made him the ideal exemplar of the broader identity he was involved in making and remaking. Importantly, while much leadership literature suggests that fairness is a key aspect of leadership (Haslam et al., 2011), Ferguson was extremely harsh on and unfair to individuals who diverged from in-group norms, regardless of their status within the group or team (e.g. David Beckham, Jaap Stam, or Roy Keane). However, rather than perpetrating acts of unfairness against individuals, Ferguson actively punished and excluded individuals who undermined or violated key normative features of the group. In doing so, he actively reinforced meaningful elements of the group identity when the acts of in-group members challenged or violated key norms that galvanised his squad. Thus, individuals that did not internalise the norms that Ferguson and his leadership group championed were non-prototypical and managed accordingly.

It is into this context that David Moyes arrived in 2013. One of his first acts was to sack Ferguson's core group of coaching staff (i.e. the broader

Continued

leadership group; Orr, 2014). Mike Phelan, for example, had been on the coaching staff at Manchester United – in some capacity – from 1999 to 2013 and was Ferguson's assistant from 2001 to 2013. In place of Ferguson's leadership team, Moyes's brought a trusted backroom staff from Everton. In sacking key members of Ferguson's leadership group, Moyes removed the connection to the previous set of understandings that had been cultivated by Ferguson's off-field leadership and the playing group. As discussed, it is important that new leaders, initially, act in accordance with the in-group prototype in order to establish a position of legitimate social influence. However, in sacking key members of Ferguson's staff, Moyes removed a key method of learning about the shared understandings that had underpinned the success of United under Ferguson. Instead, Moyes brought with him a set of shared leadership understandings from another group that were not contextually specific or meaningful to group members. In turn, this fostered a lack of support and trust from the group that, ultimately, led to his decline.

Conclusion

Although there are stereotypical characteristics of leaders such characteristics are always perceived and interpreted in social and cultural contexts (Platow & van Knippenberg, 2001). The social identity approach provides a perspective that emphasises the importance of fostering shared understandings that group members internalise as part of their self-definition. Internalised identities foster motivation, commitment, and actions in accordance with a group's purpose. Leaders that act in a manner that accentuates shared understandings of the in-group provide a strong reference point that cultivates social influence and power that harnesses *shared features of the group*. As the social context is constantly changing, leaders need to be acutely aware of shifts in what aspects of group identity are salient at a given time. In light of this awareness, there is scope to develop leadership tactics that unite members based on meaningful shared understandings of the in-group that are specific to its social and cultural history, present situation, and group members. It is from this position that a leader can lead – not by distinguishing himself or herself from the group but by embodying the contextual features of the in-group that are desirable to members and distinctive in contrast to out-groups.

References

Bate, A. (2018). *Manchester Derby highlights City and United's contrasting fortunes*. Sky Sports.

Cialdini, R., Borden, R., Thorne, A., Walker, M., Freeman, S., & Sloan, L. (1976). Basking in reflected glory: Three (football) field studies. *Journal of Personality and Social Psychology, 34*, 366–375.

Elberse, A. (2013). Ferguson's formula. *Harvard Business Review, 91*, 116–125.

Ellemers, N., De Gilder, D., & Haslam, S. (2004). Motivating individuals and groups at work: A social identity perspective on leadership and group performance. *Academy of Management Review, 29*, 459–478.

Giessner, S., & van Knippenberg, D. (2008). "License to fail": Goal definition, leader group prototypicality, and perceptions of leadership effectiveness after leader failure. *Organizational Behavior and Human Decision Processes, 105*, 14–35.

Haslam, S., & Platow, M. (2007). The link between leadership and followership: How affirming social identity translates vision into action. *Personality and Social Psychology Bulletin, 27*, 1469–1479.

Haslam, S., Reicher, S., & Platow, M. (2011). *The new psychology of leadership: Identity, influence and power.* Hove: Psychology Press.

Hogg, M. (2001). A social identity theory of leadership. *Personality and Social Psychology Review, 5*, 184–200.

Hogg, M., & Terry, D. (2000). Social identity and self-categorization processes in organizational contexts. *Academy of Management Review, 25*, 121–140.

Hogg, M., van Knippenberg, D., & Rast, D. (2012). The social identity theory of leadership: Theoretical origins, research findings, and conceptual developments. *European Review of Social Psychology, 23*, 258–304.

Lalonde, R. (1992). The dynamics of group differentiation in the face of defeat. *Personality and Social Psychology Bulletin, 18*, 336–342.

Levine, M., Prosser, A., Evans, D., & Reicher, S. (2005). Identity and emergency intervention: How social group membership and inclusiveness of group boundaries shape helping behavior. *Personality and Social Psychology Bulletin, 31*, 443–453.

Lock, D., & Heere, B. (2017). Identity crisis: A theoretical analysis of 'team identification' research. *European Sport Management Quarterly, 17*, 413–435.

Oakes, P., Turner, J., & Haslam, S. (1991). Perceiving people as group members: The role of fit in the salience of social categorizations. *British Journal of Social Psychology, 30*, 125–144.

Orr, J. (2014). *David Moyes sacked: 10 reasons why it has gone so wrong for the manager at Manchester United.* Independent.

Platow, M., & van Knippenberg, D. (2001). A social identity analysis of leadership endorsement: The effects of leader ingroup prototypicality and distributive intergroup fairness. *Personality and Social Psychology Bulletin, 27*, 1508–1519.

Reed, A. (2002). Social identity as a useful perspective for self concept–based consumer research. *Psychology and Marketing, 19*, 235–266.

Reicher, S., & Hopkins, N. (1996). Self-category constructions in political rhetoric; an analysis of Thatcher's and Kinnock's speeches concerning the British miners' strike (1984–5). *European Journal of Social Psychology, 26*, 353–371.

Reicher, S., Haslam, S., & Hopkins, N. (2005). Social identity and the dynamics of leadership: Leaders and followers as collaborative agents in the transformation of social reality. *Leadership Quotes, 16*, 547–568.

Reicher, S., Spears, R., & Haslam, S. (2010). The social identity approach in social psychology. In M. Wetherell & C. Talpade Mohanty (Eds.), *The Sage handbook of identities* (pp. 45–62). Sage: London.

Robson, J. (2018). Manchester United manager Jose Mourinho claims there's a reason for Pep Guardiola's success *Manchester Evening News*, May 1. Retrieved from https://www.manchestereveningnews.co.uk/sport/football/football-news/jose-mourinho-title-pep-guardiola-14600318.

Shilbury, D., Quick, S., Westerbeek, H., Funk, D., & Karg, A. (2014). *Strategic sport marketing*. Crows Nest: Allen & Unwin.

Tajfel, H., & Turner, J. (1979). An integrative theory of intergroup conflict. In W. Austin & S. Worchel (Eds.), *The Social Psychology of Intergroup Relations* (pp. 33–47). Monterey: Brooks/Cole Publishing Company.

Turner, J. (1982). Towards a cognitive redefinition of the social group. In H. Tajfel (Ed.), *Social identity and intergroup relations, European studies in social psychology* (pp. 15–40). Cambridge: Cambridge University Press.

Turner, J. (2005). Explaining the nature of power: A three process theory. *European Journal of Social Psychology, 35*, 1–22.

Turner, J., & Brown, R. (1978). Social status, cognitive alternatives and intergroup relations. In H. Tajfel (Ed.), *Differentiation between social groups: Studies in the social psychology of intergroup relations* (pp. 201–234). London: Academic Press.

Turner, J., Hogg, M., Oakes, P., Reicher, S., & Wetherell, M. (1987). *Rediscovering the social group: A self-categorization theory*. London: Blackwell.

Turner, J., Reynolds, K., & Subasic, E. (2008). Identity confers power: The new view of leadership in social psychology. In P. Hart & J. Uhr (Eds.), *Public leadership: Perspectives and practices* (pp. 57–72). Canberra: ANU.

Tyler, B., & Cobbs, J. (2017). All rivals are not equal: Clarifying misrepresentations and discerning three core properties of rivalry. *Journal of Sport Management, 31*, 1–14.

3 Developing leaders and planning succession in sport organisations

Introduction

While the study of leadership has grown to be a wide and deep area of research within the broader field of management studies the focus on how leaders are best developed is still relatively unknown (Avolio, 2011; Bryman, 2011; Yukl, 1989). Research into how leaders can be developed has been progressing though over the past 40 years; however this body of work suggests that the area of study is more complicated than it appears (Bass, 1995; Day, Fleenor, Atwater, Sturm, & McKee, 2014; DeRue & Wellman, 2009). The study of leadership development has gathered importance more recently as the realisation that strong and effective leaders provide a source of advantage for all types of organisations and businesses (Day, 2001). Another crucial aspect of leadership development is the relationship it has with succession management (Day et al., 2014). Organisations need not only develop their own leadership talent – they must also plan how that talent will be transitioned within their organisations over the mid- to longer term (Avolio & Gardner, 2005).

While the leadership development research literature has been growing in recent years, albeit at a slower pace than the generic leadership field, the application of this body of research to the field of sport management has been virtually non-existent. While sport has been a valuable setting for the conduct of organisational research, it is very surprising that more leadership and leadership development studies have not been completed (Fletcher & Wagstaff, 2009; Wolfe et al., 2005). Furthermore, this is in the context of the significant globalisation and commercialisation of sport over the past five decades and the enormous pressure placed on those who hold leadership positions in sport (Fletcher & Arnold, 2015).

Today, senior management, board members, coaches, and captains not only face intense media scrutiny but must also attain the high standards expected from critical stakeholders such as sponsors, broadcasters, general media, the wider community, and fans.

Conducting research and developing a deeper understanding of leadership development in the complex sport industry provides an opportunity for advancement of our knowledge in what will only become an increasingly important field of study (Ferkins & Shilbury, 2012; Kellet, 1999; Marjoribanks & Farquharson, 2016; Shilbury & Ferkins, 2011).

Leadership development and sport management

Despite being a large and fast-growing area of research within the broader field of management, the study of leadership development from a sport management perspective is surprisingly minimal (Frawley, Favaloro, & Schulenkorf 2018). Any research that has been completed from this perspective has primarily been centred on athletes and coaches with little focus on sport managers. Some examples of these types of studies include research that has explored leadership programmes in high schools for athletes, finding that for these programmes to work well the facilitators need to provide students with a degree of control and responsibility for the programmes and how they are managed (Blanton, Sturges, & Gould 2014); from an elite collegiate perspective the work of Voight (2012) found that structured leadership development programmes were beneficial for helping teams meet the goals they set for their competitive season; within a similar type of setting the work of Bucci, Bloom, Loughead, and Caron (2012) investigated coaches' perception of athlete leadership, finding that the empowerment of athletes through increased responsibility and decision-making improved the relationships between both parties.

Writing from a sport management perspective Westerbeek and Smith (2005) have suggested that the context of elite sport demonstrates the importance of continual learning, research, development, and innovation that can be applied to all types of organisations. When applied to the business of sport, leadership development programmes and strategies should therefore consider the importance of continual development, learning, and innovation in order to maximise employee and organisational outcomes. Despite these suggestions and as highlighted by the work of Frawley, Favaloro, & Schulenkorf (2018) the implementation of leadership development within sport organisations has been underutilised.

Leadership development

According to McCauley, Moxley, and Van Veslor (1998) leadership development can be described as "expanding the collective capacity of organisational members to engage effectively in leadership roles and processes" (p. 10). How, though, does leadership development differ from management development? Day (2001) suggests that management development is more focussed on managerial training and education with attention on specific skill acquisition and knowledge to improve task performance. Leadership development, on the other hand, targets the enhancement of human, social, and emotional capital in order for managers to engage better in leadership-related roles, tasks, and processes (McCauley, DeRue, Yost, & Taylor, 2013).

The work of Fulmer and Bleak (2008) investigated leadership development from a best practice viewpoint and found that four central benchmarks were common when attempting to understand the implementation of leadership development in organisations. These included making leadership a strategic lever, aligning strategy and leadership development, implementing successful strategic leadership development, and evaluating successful strategic leadership development. It also argued that senior management teams must be heavily engaged in the setting up and total oversight of leadership development programmes in their organisations, and not only left to the human resource department to manage.

Supporting this perspective Miller and Desmarais (2007) have stated that leadership development strategies delivered from the top of organisations will provide a better fit with the overall vision and strategic direction of the firm. This viewpoint is important because organisations need to align their broader objectives with their leadership development objectives, therefore placing leadership development at the core of the organisation's strategy (Fulmer & Bleak, 2008). The leadership development that is supported by the top management team will therefore avoid the common problem of being viewed as part of the human resource management 'silo' structure. Leadership development that is considered a strategic priority for an organisation and is ongoing rather than a one-off event will have a better chance of achieving alignment between the development needs of the organisation and its top management team (Miller & Desmarais, 2007).

Experience-based leadership development

A sub-discipline of leadership development that has emerged over the past couple of decades is known as experience-based leadership development. This approach is driven by the core idea that experience is the best teacher (DeRue & Wellman, 2009; McCall, 2010; Thomas, 2008a; 2008b; Thomas & Cheese, 2005; Yeung & Ready, 1995). According to Andresen, Boud, and Cohen (2001) such an approach is learner- and participation-centred, with a strong emphasis on "direct engagement, rich learning events and the construction of meaning" by leaders themselves (p. 225). As outlined by Thomas (2008a), the experience-based approach thereby brings together "life experiences, on the job experience, and specific skill development, stimulating reflection on experience and openness towards continuous learning" (p. 14). It is important to note, though, that experience-based leadership development is not an automatic occurrence as people learn in different ways and across different time frames, therefore making such an approach to leadership development a challenge to implement (Trautmann, Maher, & Motley, 2007). Evidence of this is when employees with leadership talent are fast-tracked into leadership roles and then struggle to achieve due to the fact that they have mainly had success in their young careers and have had little experience learning and recovering from failure (Trautmann et al., 2007).

Time therefore is an important feature of the experience-based approach. "Key moments in time, including company milestones or the recovery from failure, present opportunities for reflections of the status quo – also from a leadership perspective" (Frawley, Favaloro, & Schulenkorf, 2018). Fulmer and Bleak (2008) argue that leaders who experience major change events or incidents have the opportunity to use them to create profound teachable moments. As Thomas (2008b) has outlined, critical events can be "an utterly transforming period of testing from which one can emerge either hopelessly broken or powerfully embodied to learn and to lead" (p. 3). Developing leaders, then, can be described as a complex thing in that it rarely occurs in the classroom; instead, the deepest lessons come from personal crucible events (Thomas, 2008a).

These ideas are in close alignment with the work of McCall (2010), who has argued that experience-based leadership development approaches should be maximised in organisations through their day-to-day operations. Leadership development, therefore, becomes focussed on the interaction between the individual and the social and organisational context in which they are situated. Based on significant research involving many leading organisations McCall (2010) has proposed the seven 'sure bets' about the role of experience in leadership development:

> 1) To the extent it is learned, leadership is learned from experience; 2) Certain experiences matter more than others; 3) These experiences are powerful because of the challenges they present; 4) Different types of experiences teach different lessons; 5) Jobs and assignments can be made more developmental; 6) People can get many of the experiences they need in spite of the obstacles; and 7) Learning takes place over time and is dynamic.
>
> (p. 3)

The question, though, should be why so many organisations fail to apply these 'sure bets'? McCall (2010) suggests that the reasons for this include senior management's singular focus on the drive for results in association with the lack of understanding about leadership development by senior human resource management professionals. Human resource professionals in this sense often have a very narrow perspective about leadership development and exert too much control over the process. To counter this lack of impact McCall (2010) suggests a framework for fostering leadership talent that includes: "a) Determine what needs to be learnt; b) Identify experiences that could offer those lessons; c) Find a way to get the needed experiences; and d) Create the necessary feedback, support, and incentives to actually learn the lessons sought" (p. 14).

Organisations should therefore create 'developmental work' that is conducive to learning (Nyhan, Cressey, Tomassini, Kelleher, & Poell, 2004). When employees undertake challenging tasks the developmental value is increased when quality feedback and support is provided over time to ensure that the experience is fully leveraged (Trautmann et al., 2007). People who can learn from a broad range of experiences, who actively seek learning, and who can develop a range of skills for responding to different opportunities are generally the most effective learners (McCall, 2010). When organisations embrace this style of on the job learning and developmental opportunities leadership talent can be truly fostered (McCall, 2010).

Case study – leadership development and professional sport in Australia

Based on research conducted by scholars from the UTS Business School in Sydney, six leading Australian sport stakeholders took part in a study exploring leadership development practices starting in 2012 and finishing in 2016. The organisations involved included four of the biggest sport governing bodies in Australia, the leading sport media company, and one of the country's biggest sponsors of sport. Across the broader study 30 more senior executives, including CEOs, Deputy CEOs, and Chief Operating Officers, were interviewed. The following is a brief discussion on one part of the findings dealing with experience-based leadership development specifically in relation to the sport governing bodies.

In attempting to understand how the national governing bodies deployed experience-based leadership within their organisations four main themes emerged from the in-depth interviews. These included (1) the importance of experience-based opportunities for leadership development, (2) how experience can lead to leadership development through involvement and exposure, (3) networking opportunities that arose through experience-based exposure, and (4) the relationship between experience and education for leadership development.

Importance of experience

- Each organisation valued the development and learning opportunities that on the job experience provided for their staff.
- Rather than one single important experience being crucial for the development of leaders, it was found that a series of experiences and critical events over time provided leaders with greater confidence and knowledge.
- Learning through failure was regarded as an important aspect of how leaders developed, with respondents suggesting that the self-awareness gained from poor decision-making can make leaders more confident when dealing with similar matters in the future. As outlined by one respondent:

People shouldn't be scared of their experiences because we all make mistakes and have a few failures, but that's how you learn … At the end of it, through those few mistakes, you have profited from a learning side of it.

Continued

Development through involvement and exposure

Experience-based opportunities were found to be a positive feature of the participant's development due to the exposure and involvement they gained via tasks and assignments that stretched their skills and knowledge. This view was endorsed by all the organisations that took part in the study.

The respondents highlighted the aforementioned process as critical to their own development and growth throughout their careers. As outlined by one interviewee:

> The most significant part of my development has been through the opportunity to work on projects ... what [the CEO] does ... he has the confidence ... to give you projects ... that might well be of significant scope and let you have a crack at it ... The fact that they done that and have the confidence in you means you are able to progress because they have given you the opportunity.

Experience-based projects and tasks were an important part of employee development according to the respondents as this type of exposure and involvement was crucial in building confidence and knowledge. This approach allowed individuals to put into practice the skills learned in more formal classroom activities and then to form new abilities from the developmental experiences.

Networking opportunities through exposure

Experience-based leadership development practices were found to provide opportunities for exposure and networking.

Participants outlined how their exposure to experience-based leadership provided access to new contacts and industry leaders. As outlined by a participant, "being exposed to many different groups of people ... we have such strong networks, and to some very great community leaders and business leaders, you learn by just working alongside those people".

Exposure to internal leaders was also mentioned as an important feature of the experience-based approach to leadership development, allowing individuals to prove themselves and to make a name for themselves with key internal people.

Such experiences can help future leaders to form internal and external contacts that will be beneficial for learning and mentoring opportunities and also future employment prospects.

Partnership between experience and education

Only one of the governing bodies involved in the study had both a mix of experience-based leadership development with detailed processes for external formal education.

This organisation viewed both elements as part of a broader holistic approach to leadership development. As outlined by a senior executive, "they go hand in glove … it is very hard to have one without the other to really progress to the top levels (of the organisation)".

The leading governing body in Australia based on financial turnover and media exposure demonstrated that it was necessary to provide a well-rounded leadership development programme that was heavily influenced by experience-based approaches but also complemented with formal education opportunities such as executive programmes at Stanford University and Harvard University.

Discussion

According to McCall (2010) experience-based leadership development works best when organisations determine what needs to be learned; identify experiences that can offer those lessons; find a way to get those required experiences; and establish the necessary feedback, support, and motivation to ensure that the lessons sought are actually learned. To achieve this sporting organisations should create individual leadership plans for each employee. Such plans will help employees understand where they sit and how they can get to the next level in their leadership development within the organisation with the necessary support provided. This process provides clarity and transparency for all staff. In highly successful companies, leadership development is deeply embedded through processes, programmes, and systems designed to support the workforce (McCauley & McCall, 2014). Through such systems and policies leadership development becomes ingrained and therefore part of the organisation's culture.

In alignment with McCall's (2010) third point sport organisations should provide engaging experiences to enhance the leadership development process. The study of Australia's leading professional sport organisations showed that they each actively used experience-based opportunities to expose their workforce to challenging tasks and experiences (Frawley, Favaloro, & Schulenkorf, 2018). This approach is one of the most effective ways to maximise leadership development in the day-to-day work setting (McCall, 2010). While this approach is desirable many organisations do find it challenging, especially if resources are scarce.

The final aspect of the McCall (2010) framework is providing the required support, feedback, and incentives to ensure that the sport organisation workforce can learn and grow from the experiences they partake in. In this way it enriches the experience so that the workforce reflects deeply on the learning that takes place in order to make adjustments for future projects and activities. When challenging tasks are provided and then discussed and assessed with adequate support and feedback, meaningful development can take place (DeRue & Wellman, 2009). The challenge here for senior management is to balance the structure that is required in order to fully assess the development activities while also having sufficient flexibility to embrace unforeseen or unplanned consequences that can arise (McCauley & McCall, 2014).

Conclusion

For sport organisations to maximise their productivity and performance they need to create developmental work that is conducive to learning (Nyhan et al., 2004). When people are given challenging tasks to complete that are supported in a learning environment with detailed feedback processes and related support leadership, development is maximised (Trautmann et al., 2007). Leaders who develop strong capacity are often those who have had the opportunity to learn from a broad range of experiences and who seek out new learning challenges (Nyhan et al., 2004). For leadership development to be successfully implemented it must also be a shared responsibility between the workforce and the sport organisation – senior management including the CEO must be actively involved in the oversight of the leadership development programme (Fulmer & Bleak, 2008). It should not solely be left to the human resources department to manage and oversee. Leadership development strategies that are created at the top of the organisation provide a better fit and alignment with the broader direction and vision of the firm (Miller & Desmarais, 2007). (The case study at the end of this chapter, an interview with the President of the Australian Paralympic Committee, demonstrates how leaders can develop and change their understanding of leadership over the course of their career life cycle.)

Succession management

An important consequence of leadership development in organisations is their ability to plan leadership succession (Rothwell, 2010). The concept of succession management has been examined by management scholars for many decades now as a critical human resource process that seeks to identify suitable replacements for executives who eventually will leave their organisation due to retirement or illness (Fulmer & Conger, 2004b). For some organisations though, this process was not much more than a list of names updated over time. Today, however, in the competitive business environment not developing people internally to replace those who leave is not an adequate response (Groves, 2007). Organisations need to be more holistic in their approach by integrating leadership development with succession management for a comprehensive process that identifies future leaders at all levels (Mehrabani & Mohama, 2011). Succession management therefore can be described as a way to "facilitate effective workforce planning through the identification and development of candidates with the skills, knowledge and capabilities to fill critical roles in the organisation to achieve successful business outcomes" (Taylor & McGraw, 2004, pp. 742–743).

A well-designed succession management system should do two things: first, it needs to serve the needs of the organisation by providing an ongoing supply of talent; second, it needs to serve the employees by improving their competencies, management and leadership skills (Fulmer & Conger, 2004b). While many organisations in the past have treated succession management and leadership development as separate functions Conger and Fulmer (2003) argue that these practices need to be viewed as fully integrated processes. Succession management and leadership development are "natural allies because they share a vital and fundamental goal: getting the right skills in the right place" (Fulmer & Conger, 2004a, p. 39). A holistic approach therefore means organisations are able to develop their management teams with the skills required to lead and the workforce is able to develop their capabilities for future career advancement. Succession management system best practices should therefore comprise the following components: (1) straightforward and simple to use, (2) development focussed rather than replacement focussed, (3) involve senior management in its oversight and not leave it solely to the human resource department to manage, (4) can spot gaps in talent and identify critical positions that need to be filled, (5) designed for continual improvement and development, and (6) constantly evaluating the process to ensure that the right people are moving into the right positions (Fulmer & Conger, 2004b).

Succession management in sport

Not unlike the leadership development literature the research completed on succession management with a sport industry focus has been limited. The research that has been conducted into leadership succession in sport has mainly centred on professional sport coaches, generally from a North American perspective (e.g. Giambatista, Rowe, & Riaz, 2005; Soebbing & Washington, 2011). These studies have largely examined the impact of managerial succession on club franchise and elite sporting performance. Meanwhile, our knowledge on the succession management practices within sport organisations to identify and develop future leaders for senior executive roles is still underdeveloped.

Taylor, Doherty, and McGraw (2008) have been one of the few to explore succession management from a sports perspective, highlighting that a sport organisation's approach to succession management should be guided by its strategic objectives, environmental context, and human resource needs. This viewpoint suggests that while there are some key components that are common amongst effective succession management systems, ultimately, different organisations will have their own requirements depending on the context.

Case study – succession management and professional sport in Australia

Succession management was regarded as an important process by the participating sport organisations. Executives from the sport organisations that took part in the study suggested that their succession management provided their businesses with stability and a sense of continuity. While the significance of succession management was acknowledged by the senior executives interviewed the manner in which it was implemented varied across the three organisations.

Only one of the organisations that took part in the study had a well-developed succession management system linked to a leadership development programme. This organisation had a holistic approach with a clear succession structure across various levels of the organisation. In addition to the senior management team a second team of approximately ten managers referred to as the outer executive had been identified as the potential individuals to fill the gap if those above them left the organisation. The outer executive provided a clear pathway for progression in the organisation and linked to the leadership development strategy, including experience-based stretch projects and formal education opportunities. Having a clear succession structure had the advantage of providing transparency for those in the organisation and what they were required to do in order to rise to the senior executive team.

The leading organisation in this study and one of Australia's largest governing bodies demonstrated that its greatest strength was its holistic approach to leadership development and succession management. This holistic structure integrated leadership development and succession management practices together into a comprehensive process used for identifying and preparing future leaders for their organisation (Conger & Fulmer, 2003; Fulmer & Conger, 2004a; Groves, 2007). The clear and transparent structure enabled the organisation to identify and develop those with talent to produce competent and successful leaders. The fact that this organisation has produced its CEO talent from within, whilst other comparable organisations have recruited externally is another sign of their succession management success.

Conclusion

In summary, the management literature demonstrates that succession management and leadership development practices need to reflect the specific context of their organisations. Further research though is required to deepen our knowledge of these processes within sport organisations. Research into succession management within the global sport industry also provides scholars with the potential to broaden our understanding of leadership development.

Case study – an interview with Mr Glenn Tasker, President of the Australian Paralympic Committee and former CEO of Swimming Australia

Conducted by Dr Stephen Frawley

STEPHEN: *"Glenn, I am interested in how senior managers who work for sport organisations develop their view of leadership and how it changes overtime. Did your view of leadership, and what it meant to be a good leader, change much overtime and if so what were the reasons for that change?"*

GLENN: *"No doubt. Early in my sports management career, I thought that sporting organisations boards were the leaders and that I followed their directions. It became obvious as my credibility grew that the boards, with whom I worked were looking for leadership from me. This translated into how I operated with staff, who similarly were looking for leadership not just direction. This was even more apparent when I started working with younger staff members, who were looking to build a career. I found that I became a transformational leader as most organisations with whom I took roles were looking for change".*

STEPHEN: *"Looking back at your career in sport, what do you think are the central characteristics that have shaped your leadership?"*

GLENN: *"Every role I had was with a sport which was not familiar to me. I had no real knowledge of the sports or how they operated from a game point of view or a governance post of view. Having a "fresh outlook" was a great benefit to me. Often those close to a sport cannot be objective enough to make hard decisions or to change. Similarly, my employers wanted change and they were happy to teach me the sport. In many ways, this allowed me to make changes with the sports' imprimatur when I had credibility with directors, coaches and clubs".*

STEPHEN: *"What have been some of the key characteristics that have shaped the successful leaders you have worked for or with in sport?"*

GLENN: *"I think there are six key characteristics: 1. They have had empathy with people; 2. They are good listeners; 3. They are trustworthy; 4. They have self-confidence; 5. They have tenacity; and, 6. They lead by example".*

STEPHEN: *"What advice would you give to young sport administrators setting out on their careers to help them develop their leadership skills?"*

GLENN: *"First, understand what leadership is and what it is not. Let this help you determine what kind of leader you wish to be. Second, learn from good leaders and from bad ones; knowing what not to do is just as important as knowing what to do. Third, avoid office politics: Machiavellian types do not work in modern societies except maybe in real politics! Fourth, be ethical. Fifth, be part of a team; lone workers end up with*

Continued

> lonely tasks. Teamwork can overcome many adversities. Sixth, develop conflict resolution skills: peace makers are better than war mongers. Finally, develop strategic thinking skills: leaders need to set strategy as well as deliver it".
>
> STEPHEN: "Thanks for your time, Glenn".

References

Andresen, L., Boud, D., & Cohen, R. (2001). Experience-based learning. In G. Foley (Ed.), *Understanding adult education and training* (2nd ed., pp. 225–239). Sydney: Allen & Unwin.

Avolio, B. J. (2011). *Full range leadership development* (2nd ed.). Thousand Oaks, CA: Sage.

Avolio, B. J., & Gardner, W. L. (2005). Authentic leadership development: Getting to the root of positive forms of leadership. *Leadership Quarterly, 16*(1), 315–338.

Bass, B. M. (1995). *Leadership and performance beyond expectations.* New York: Free Press.

Blanton, J. E., Sturges, A. J., & Gould, D. (2014). Lessons learned from a leadership development club for high school athletes. *Journal of Sport Psychology in Action, 5*(1), 1–13.

Bryman, A. (2011). Mission accomplished? Research methods in the first five years of leadership. *Leadership, 7*(1), 73–83.

Bucci, J., Bloom, G. A., Loughead, T. M., & Caron, J. G. (2012). Ice hockey coaches' perceptions of athlete leadership. *Journal of Applied Sport Psychology, 24*(3), 243–259.

Conger, J. A., & Fulmer, R. M. (2003). Developing your leadership pipeline. *Harvard Business Review, 81*(12), 76–90.

Day, D. V. (2001). Leadership development: A review in context. *Leadership Quarterly, 11*(4), 581–613.

Day, D. V., Fleenor, J. W., Atwater, L. E., Sturm, R. E., & McKee, R. A. (2014). Advances in leader and leadership development: A review of 25 years of research and theory. *The Leadership Quarterly, 25*(1), 63–82.

DeRue, D. S., & Wellman, N. (2009). Developing leaders via experience: The role of developmental challenge, learning orientation, and feedback availability. *Journal of Applied Psychology, 94*(4), 859.

Ferkins, L., & Shilbury, D. (2012). Good boards are strategic: What does that mean for sport governance? *Journal of Sport Management, 26*(1), 67–80.

Fletcher, D., & Arnold, R. (2015). Performance leadership and management in elite sport: Current status and future directions. In S. Andersen, B. Houlihan, & L. T. Ronglan (Eds.), *Managing elite sport systems: Research and practice* (pp. 162–181). Abingdon: Routledge.

Frawley, S., Favaloro, D., & Schulenkorf, N. (2018). Experience-based leadership development and professional sport organizations. *Journal of Sport Management, 32*(2), 123–134.

Fletcher, D., & Wagstaff, C. R. D. (2009). Organisational psychology in elite sport: Its emergence, application and future. *Psychology of Sport and Exercise, 10*, 427–434.

Fulmer, R. M., & Bleak, J. L. (2008). *The leadership advantage: How the best companies are developing their talent to pave the way for future success.* New York: AMACON.

Fulmer, R. M., & Conger, J. A. (2004a). Developing leaders with 2020 vision. *Financial Executive, 20*(5), 38–41.

Fulmer, R. M., & Conger, J. A. (2004b). *Growing your company's leaders: How great organisations use succession management to maintain competitive advantage.* New York: AMACON.

Giambatista, R. C., Rowe, W. G., & Riaz, S. (2005). Nothing succeeds like succession: A critical review of leader succession literature since 1994. *The Leadership Quarterly, 16*(1), 963–991.

Groves, K. S. (2007). Integrating leadership development and succession planning best practices. *Journal Management Development, 26*(3), 239–260.

Kellet, P. (1999). Organisational leadership: Lessons from professional coaches. *Sport Management Review, 2*(1), 150–171.

Marjoribanks, T., & Farquharson, K. (2016). Contesting competence: Chief executive officers and leadership in Australian Football League clubs. *Marketing Intelligence & Planning, 34*(2), 188–202.

McCall, M. W. (2010). Recasting leadership development. *Industrial Organisational Psychology, 3*(1), 3–19.

McCauley, C. D., DeRue, D. S., Yost, P. R., & Taylor, S. (2013). *Experience-driven leader development: Models, tools, best practices, and advice for on-the-job development.* San Francisco, CA: John Wiley & Sons.

McCauley, C. D., & McCall, M. W. (2014). *Using experience to develop leadership talent: How organizations leverage on-the-job development.* London: John Wiley & Sons.

McCauley, C. D., Moxley, R. S., & Van Veslor, E. (1998). *The center for creative leadership handbook of leadership development.* San Francisco, CA: Jossey-Bass Publishing.

Mehrabani, S. E., & Mohamad, N. A. (2011). Succession planning: A necessary process in today's organisation. *International Journal of e-Education, e-Management & e-Learning, 1*(5), 371–377.

Miller, D., & Desmarais, S. (2007). Developing your talent to the next level: Five best practices for leadership development. *Organisational Development Journal, 25*(3), 37–43.

Nyhan, B., Cressey, P., Tomassini, M., Kelleher, M., & Poell, R. (2004). European perspectives on the learning organisation. *Journal of European Industrial Training, 28*(1), 67–92.

Rothwell, W. J. (2010). *Effective succession management: Ensuring leadership continuity & building talent from within*, 4th ed. New York: AMACON.

Shilbury, D., & Ferkins, L. (2011). Professionalisation, sport governance and strategic capability. *Managing Leisure, 16*(2), 108–127.

Soebbing, B. P., & Washington, M. (2011). Leadership succession and organizational performance: Football coaches and organizational issues. *Journal of Sport Management, 25*(6), 550–561.

Taylor, T., Doherty, A., & McGraw, P. (2008). *Managing people in sport organisations: A strategic human resource management perspective.* Oxford: Butterworth-Heinemann.

Taylor, T., & McGraw, P. (2004). Succession management practices in Australian organisations. *International Journal of Manpower, 25*(8), 741–758.

Thomas, R. J. (2008a). Crucibles of leadership development. *Sloan Management Review, 49*(3), 14–18.

Thomas, R. J. (2008b). *Crucibles of leadership: How to learn from experience to become a great leader.* Boston, MA: Harvard Business Press.

Thomas, R. J., & Cheese, P. (2005). Leadership: Experience is the best teacher. *Strategy and Leadership, 33*(3), 24–29.

Trautmann, K., Maher, J. K., & Motley, D. G. (2007). Learning strategies as predictors of transformational leadership: The case of nonprofit managers. *Leadership and Organisational Development Journal, 28*(3), 269–287.

Voight, M. (2012). A leadership development intervention program: A case study with two elite teams. *The Sport Psychologist, 26*(4), 604–623.

Westerbeek, H., & Smith, A. (2005). *Business leadership and the lessons from sport.* New York: Palgrave Macmillan.

Wolfe, R. A., Weick, K. E., Usher, J. M., Terborg, J. R., Poppo, L., Murrell, A. J., & Simmons Jourdan, J. (2005). Sport and organisational studies. *Journal of Management Inquiry, 14*(2), 182–210.

Yeung, A. K., & Ready, D. A. (1995). Developing leadership capabilities of global corporations: A comparative study in eight nations. *Human Resource Management, 34*(4), 529–547.

Yukl, G. (1989). Managerial leadership: A review of theory and research. *Journal of Management, 15*(2), 251–289.

4 Cross-border leadership and the management of sport

Introduction

In the twentieth century, an important shift was witnessed in the international business world, from looking at and caring about 'management' towards an emphasis on 'leadership'. While this shift appears subtle, the difference in meaning is significant. According to Bird and Mendenhall (2016), the term management was used frequently in the pre-1960s business literature, where the operational focus was predominantly task-oriented. In other words, there was an emphasis on maintaining a certain style of business practice without innovation or entrepreneurial desires for transformative change. As economies and politics became more global, more multicultural, and more complex in nature, change and transformation were inevitable, and the North American hegemony of managerial business practice soon came under scrutiny. What was needed, in an increasingly global and ever-shifting world, was less management and more leadership – leadership that could create a vision, instigate change, cross borders, and react to an increasingly complex playing field.

As part of the global business world, the sport industry has embraced leadership studies since the 1970s. Since then, sport management scholars have tackled leadership debates from diverse angles and in a variety of contexts. As discussed throughout this book, many theoretical and empirical advances have been made, including investigations into different leadership styles and behaviours and their relationship with micro, meso, and macro outcomes. However, according to Welty Peachey et al. (2015), the majority of sport leadership research to date explores the on-the-field leadership of sport teams (e.g. coaches and their teams), rather than the organisational off-field leadership components related to sport management. In this chapter, we focus on a particularly challenging off-field aspect of sport leadership: namely leadership across borders. While leadership per se is considered a complex managerial phenomenon, this is particularly relevant for sport leadership that is conducted across geographical, sociocultural, political, generational, structural, sporting, and/or organisational borders. Here, sport leaders confront additional challenges in a dynamic and ever-changing environment.

In this chapter, we first introduce the field of cross-border leadership and propose a new and inclusive working definition. This definition provides the background to our discussion of the specific traits and competencies of cross-border leaders. Next, we explore specific challenges and future opportunities for cross-border leadership. As part of this exploration, we refer to current research in international settings – including different cross-border case studies and reflections from a Pacific Islands context that illustrate the complex nature of leadership across sporting and cultural divides.

From global leadership to leadership across borders: towards a working definition

Our starting point for the discussion of cross-border leadership is the phenomenon of globalisation. In short, in the twenty-first century, sporting organisations are operating and competing in an increasingly global marketplace. Since the 1990s, international interactions have become the norm for professional sport organisations and businesses; in fact, Bird and Mendenhall (2016) remarked that since that time, international relationships have advanced from being unilateral exchanges to multinational engagements, with the world being "more non-linear in nature" (p. 118). In short, the sporting world has become more complex to manage, and global leaders have been faced with significant tasks and challenges.

Increased complexity and the associated diversification of leadership assignments have led to an ever-growing body of research on global leadership. However, defining 'global leadership' has been a complicated task, given the vague ways in which the terminology has been used in different studies (e.g. Bird & Mendenhall, 2016; Jokinen, 2005; Mendenhall, Reiche, Bird, & Osland, 2012). There are those who describe a global leader qua position or role, such as an executive or manager with global responsibilities (see Jokinen, 2005; McCall & Hollenbeck, 2002). A more technical definition is supplied by Caligiuri and Tarique (2009), who state that global leaders are "high level professionals such as executives, vice presidents, directors and managers who are in jobs with some global leadership activities such as global integration responsibilities" (p. 336). This definition adds a task-based element to the mix; it also assumes that leaders hold specific high-positioned jobs within an organisation. However, other scholars argue that this may not have to be the case. In fact, as Jokinen (2005) points out (as alluded to in Chapter 2), global leadership may also be found in lower levels of an organisation's hierarchy and may not have to be linked to official positions of power.

While the global leadership literature has understandably focussed on the geographical aspects of cross-border leadership, in this chapter we refer to cross-border leadership as more than merely an engagement across countries. Instead, cross-border leadership is seen holistically and may also include managerial responsibilities across sociocultural, political (portfolios), generational, structural, sporting, organisational, and other borders. All these aspects are relevant for sport leaders in the twenty-first century, where businesses and not-for-profit sport organisations are trying to find a balance between growth, expansion, and internationalisation on the one hand and community focus, local engagement, and social responsibility on the other hand.

While in the past, the terms 'global', 'cross-cultural', and 'cross-border' have often been used interchangeably, we argue that a more specific definition is needed to clearly distinguish between the concepts and their foci. In regard to cross-border leadership, this is particularly important given our holistic under-standing of different (hard and soft) borders that exist in today's business world. In addressing this issue, we put forward an encompassing working definition for this chapter and define cross-border leadership as:

> an inclusive and dynamic process of listening, learning, challenging, influ-encing, guiding, and motivating others across diverse contexts and back-grounds with the intent of leading them towards a relevant, meaningful, and coherent goal.

Cross-border leadership traits and competencies

In line with the working definition provided earlier – and with a focus on achieving desired goals and outcomes – cross-border leaders build on certain traits, competencies, and/or attributes that help them fulfil their mission. These include cross-cultural skills or what Rosen and Digh (quoted in Alon & Higgens, 2005) have described as 'global literacy', which means "seeing, thinking, acting and mobilising in culturally mindful ways" (p. 503). The authors suggest that global literacy encompasses four types of competencies, namely:

1. **Personal literacy.** Understanding and valuing oneself, evaluating and con-sistently seeking to grow as a person, being able to listen to others and take on advice while staying true to one's own beliefs.
2. **Social literacy.** Being able to engage with and challenge others, listening to and responding to the demands of the business and co-workers/fol-lowers and encouraging greater performance without damaging relation-ships or morale. Being able to use the diverse skills of others in a common purpose.
3. **Business literacy.** Being able to focus, guide, and mobilise others through business, local, or world political or economic changes. Developing leaders throughout the organisation, and understanding and harnessing the busi-ness' geography, technical aspects, systems, etc.
4. **Cultural literacy.** Understanding and leveraging cultural differences. Valuing one's own heritage while understanding its shortcomings and look-ing beyond one's own culture for opportunities and resources. Using the best of multiple cultures and being able to form relationships and alliances across cultures.

Taken together, global literacy skills will assist cross-border leaders to master their complex socio-managerial challenges, including expanding overseas businesses, conceiving strategies on a global level, dealing with conflicting constituencies, and motivating and managing geographically and culturally diverse teams (see also Caligiuri & Tarique, 2009). Against this background, we suggest that the most effective way to increase global literacy and cross-border leadership skills is to have extensive and immersive experiences in other business and/or sociocultural contexts, including through workplace initiatives or as part of an individual's own life experiences or interests (see also Alon & Higgens, 2005; Caligiuri & Tarique, 2009; Rockstuhl et al., 2011). Again, immersion is not limited to geographical contexts but also includes experiences with other (working) cultures, political environments, age groups, sporting codes, organisational setups, and so on. Finally, with international settings, the willingness and ability to address language barriers is another significant competency of a cross-border leader. While the business world often uses English as its dominant language, Youseff and Lutham (2012) acknowledge that there is more to a language than just literal translations. A 'positive leader' would appreciate the intrinsic value of language to cultural groups and try to learn or engage with new languages – or at least appreciate others who have experience and expertise in foreign languages. Overall, it can be surmised that the exposure to – and engagement with – unfamiliar contexts presents a challenging but promising way in which the outlook, skills, and behaviours of cross-border leaders can be enriched.

In addition to the important qualities listed earlier, one often ignored aspect of leadership studies – and one that is particularly challenging when leading across borders – is the necessity of making and communicating 'dark' decisions. In this context, Cruickshank and Collins (2016, p. 1200) recently observed that most sport research is "overly absorbed with defining who effective leaders are and what they do overtly, rather than why or how they lead in a certain way at a certain time" (see Chapter 2 for further discussion). Specifically, they argued that most research has overstated the "'bright' (or socially desirable) side of leaders, at the expense of investigating the 'darker' (or socially undesirable) decisions that are clearly prevalent and effective in real world sport" (p. 2000). By 'darker' decisions they mean actions that are intended to bring, above all, benefits to the leader and his/her organisation through actions and goals that may come at the expense of others. The authors argue that 'bright' and 'dark' characteristics and behaviour patterns are often interconnected, and competency in managing both are required for effective leadership. For instance, if a coach wants to replace or demote a top player (a 'dark' goal), she may specifically encourage and support junior players to improve their performance and become more competitive and influential. Or, conversely, a coach may transfer, fire, or bench a player to increase competitiveness or secure team cohesion overall. Overall, leaders cannot and should not always be 'nice', as difficult decisions have to be made. Such difficult decisions can be particularly challenging when working across different geographical, cultural, organisational, or sporting borders, where negative feedback or rejection is perceived and managed differently depending on the social norms and values of a particular place (e.g. Barnlund & Araki, 1985; Sato, Yuki, & Norasakkunkit, 2014). Hence, the skill of making, communicating, and navigating 'dark' decisions is a key competency for effective cross-border leaders.

Cross-border leadership challenges

Earlier in this chapter, leadership across borders was given a broad and encompassing working definition. Against that background, this section will focus on discussing a number of key challenges related to cross-border leadership, specifically leadership challenges across geographical and sociocultural, generational, as well as sporting borders.

Leadership across geographical and sociocultural borders

In the context of international management, different sport organisations from around the world have been accused of not living up to the leadership standards expected and/or required of them. Examples of international leaders who fail to meet the set benchmarks in regard to sociocultural and ethical performance cut across all sectors of the sports industry, including the largest world governing bodies (e.g. International Olympic Committee, Fédération Internationale de Football Association, and International Association of Athletics Federations) and internationally operating sport-for-development (SFD) programmes. While the former receives more attention and regular scrutiny in the media, the latter deserves some more focus and interrogation when it comes to cross-border leadership. This is particularly important given the argument that "in the new, borderless economy, culture doesn't matter less; it matters more" (Rosen & Digh, 2001, p. 72).

For the past 15 years, SFD programmes have been expanding significantly all over the world (see Schulenkorf, Sherry, & Rowe, 2016 and Chapter 7 for more detail). In short, SFD initiatives use sport as a vehicle to predominantly achieve non-sporting development outcomes that can be broadly classified into seven thematic areas: Disability, Education, Gender, Health, Livelihoods, Peace, and Social Cohesion (Richards et al., 2013). Many SFD initiatives are funded and managed by sport organisations or non-governmental organisations (NGOs) from high-income countries (largely from the Global North), yet implemented in low- and middle-income countries (largely in the Global South). Acknowledging this imbalance, Lindsey and Grattan (2012) criticise traditional SFD management as "international practice undertaken in the Global South but supported, and largely driven, from the Global North" (p. 92). As this statement suggests, when leading SFD projects across countries, there are numerous challenges and risks involved. First, the combination of technical knowledge (often provided by international sport experts), as well as the cultural knowledge (provided by local communities), plays a key role in achieving relevant, meaningful, and sustainable development outcomes (e.g. Schulenkorf, 2012; Sherry, Schulenkorf, & Chalip, 2015). In other words, to avoid culturally informed assumptions, for example about the intrinsic value of sport and its capacity to achieve a range of outcomes (Coalter, 2010; Sugden, 2006), a rigorous design process and holistic engagement with stakeholders or programme partners are critical for SFD projects to deliver on their stated goals.

In their research around a healthy lifestyle SFD project in the Pacific Islands, Schulenkorf and Siefken (2019) suggested that strategic management and inclusive partnerships on the micro, meso, and macro levels can make a significant difference not only to sport programmes but also to the wider community. For this to occur, leadership in partnerships with local and international stakeholders was needed to get programmes approved and activities designed in an acceptable and productive way. In particular, strong partnerships between organisers, local communities, and external partners such as policymakers and researchers increase the likelihood of implementing, managing, communicating, leveraging, evaluating, and sustaining programmes efficiently and effectively (see also Sherry & Schulenkorf, 2016; Welty Peachey, Cohen, Shin, & Fusaro, 2018). For instance, Schulenkorf and Siefken's (2019) study showed that if sport organisations collaborate with NGOs, governmental departments, and academic providers in the rollout of new sport initiatives, different types of political, educational, and sporting leverage may be achieved. In particular, key sporting or political figures such as sport stars or ministers may come on board to support the key message of the programme, which will also help to entice the media to report on the programme's sport and non-sport activities. Clearly, fruitful cooperation between international leaders and local partners is at the heart of a successful SFD initiative.

In another positive real-life example of how SFD leadership across countries may work, Lindsey and Grattan (2012) provide evidence from Zambia, where a number of SFD organisations received international assistance without being dominated by outsiders. In fact, some of the local organisations 'owned' their sport projects and used resources rather independently. For instance, Edusport's local organising committee was empowered to 'own' and distribute finances to its local branches as it saw fit. All stakeholders confirmed that this approach was both sensible and valuable, as foreign organisations rarely know which issues the community is facing, and which focus and priorities to take specifically. In short, the hands-off approach to international leadership was perceived as empowering, as it did not force a Global North set of attitudes or cultural norms onto communities with different social and cultural backgrounds. Lindsey and Grattan's (2012) research shows that local stakeholders from Global South communities enjoy their autonomy and independence in starting and managing sport programmes. As such, the Edusport case study is an excellent example of how local communities may take the lead in identifying their own problems and coming up with solutions. For such empowering outcomes to occur, the international leaders – who are often in privileged positions – will have to engage in co-establishing a functioning local partnership framework underpinned by values such as trust, transparency, and accountability. Importantly, these values relate to both sides of the partnership, so that any unintended and damaging consequences (e.g. corruption and mis-use of funds) do not occur.

Leadership across generational borders

Leadership is often associated with older members of a group, community, or society. In fact, in the sporting world there has been much criticism that "old white men" tend to govern and dominate sporting organisations, especially at the international level. For instance, Adriaanse (2017) showed that in 2014, the global average for women's representation across International Sport Federations as board directors was 13.3%, while board chair/president was 8% and chief exec-utive/secretary-general was 21%. These findings highlight that women continue to be largely under-represented in the key leadership roles in global sport. In addition to challenges around gender equality, the aspect of cross-generational leadership becomes important in today's fast-changing world. While younger members of society may initially lack the management and governance expe-rience of their older counterparts, they provide a much-needed different (and younger) perspective on sports. The inclusion of younger voices in leadership teams is therefore critical for sport (organisations) to stay relevant, particularly in the eyes of their future market. In other words, without cross-generational lead-ership sport organisations run the risk of 'missing the mark', as they lack inno-vation and fresh ideas, thus becoming detached from their future customer base.

As such, the topics of leadership development (see Chapter 3) and succes-sion planning play an important role in the context of cross-generational lead-ership. This is particularly relevant for the many smaller sport organisations or programmes that are spearheaded by one central leader. In particular, sport-related NGOs and entrepreneurial leadership structures tend to rely heavily on an individual's status, personality, and network (Cohen & Welty Peachey, 2015; Commeh & Schulenkorf, 2008). While this may be an asset in the short and medium term, it can become problematic for the organisation's effectiveness once the leader has to be replaced. Alternatively, if a leader is 'out of touch' and perhaps not in line with the latest technological advances and media opportuni-ties, the organisation itself may struggle to stay relevant. Here, challenges arise if a leader – who is often closely connected to the cause of the NGO – is unwilling to give up power and 'cross the bridge' in an attempt to pass on responsibilities to the next generation.

The 'hanging on to power' is particularly problematic for many small-scale NGOs, where leaders are generally required to accomplish numerous roles and responsibilities at once: manage current operations, seek new opportunities, create a supportive network, embrace new technologies, develop or streamline processes, and so on. Leaders have to constantly reflect and go with the times – and all that against the background of increased competition and shoestring budgets. As most NGOs depend on external funding or grants to conduct their operations, short-term contracts and high staff turnover rates add additional complexity. 'Hanging on to power' and working with a top-down leadership approach is hardly beneficial for stakeholders, and in particular aspiring young talent who may be in a position to be developed as future leaders. As such, research into leadership and management has highlighted the challenge of a 'leadership deficit' in NGOs and the lack of resources and strategies in addressing the often insufficient pool of emerging leaders in this space.

The alleged leadership deficit can also be related to a variety of additional limitations that NGOs have been facing in an increasingly global and competitive world, including comparatively low salaries for staff, financial constraints for projects, as well as sociopolitical and cultural challenges when working with diverse communities (see Miraftab, 1997). Consequently, the questions of how to engage and develop leaders, how to keep and reward leaders, and how to transition from an old to a new generation of NGO leaders present critical challenges for the future of the sporting sector (see also Chapter 3 on Leadership Development).

Leadership across sporting borders

Sport leaders hardly work in isolation when aiming to fulfil their mission. A strong network of partners is critical when trying to plan, implement, manage, and evaluate sport initiatives. However, sport has been accused of lacking cooperation and engagement among the different codes in relation to generating and leveraging sporting outcomes. Be it for (sport) political reasons, (sport) culture, or a lack of vision, the sporting industry has arguably failed to maximise its potential from inclusive cross-discipline engagement. In other words, the lack of leadership across sporting borders has prevented sporting codes to achieve a competitive advantage through cooperation. At the same time, the lack of openness and engagement – and work in isolation – has limited creativity and innovation, and has often resulted in parallel structures that leave opportunities for leverage unused.

Case study – (lacking) leadership across sporting borders: a case study from Fiji

Dr Jack Sugden, Edge Hill University, United Kingdom

The Pacific Island nation of Fiji is a highly diverse society comprised of two main ethnic groups, Indigenous Fijians (57%) and Fijians of Indian descent (hereafter Indo-Fijians) (37%), as well as other smaller groups of mixed ethnic and other Pacific Island ancestry (Fiji Bureau of Statistics, 2015). Since independence from British rule in 1974, Fiji has struggled with its divided population, resulting in a tumultuous modern history marked by political instability and increased poverty (Lal, 2012; Robertson, 2012).

Sport in Fiji is a valuable cultural commodity, with rugby (union and sevens) occupying a place of huge significance in Indigenous culture and, by extension, the nation itself (Presterudstuen, 2010, 2016). Consequentially rugby has become a bastion of a muscular Indigenous identity, an ethnonationalist symbol, both at home and overseas (Presterudstuen & Schieder, 2016). Participation reflects this reality with rugby fields across the islands mirroring that of the army barracks and the governmental chambers in their indigeneity (Kanemausu & Molnar, 2013). As such, participation and success in rugby has become intertwined with a modern realisation of tribal culture and ordering (Presterudstuen & Schieder, 2016). At the centre of this imagining is the Fijian Rugby Union (FRU), the administrative centre of the sport, built with British paternalism and labelled by Taeiwa (2005) as 'a bastion of the Fijian (male) elite' (p. 213). The leadership and staff of the FRU are entirely Indigenous and the national rugby teams are held up as centres of the prototypical Fijian, with historical connotations linking them to a noble warrior past (Guinness & Besnier, 2016). Indeed, rugby's centrality in Fijian leadership is personified by the somewhat unique scenario of the Fijian president also sitting as the head of the FRU.

Soccer, on the other hand, provides a centre for Indo-Fijian identity. While soccer is very much backstage in Fiji in comparison with rugby, it enjoys a relatively mixed base of participation and support. However, 'football in Fiji takes on a racially charged outlook that it is an Indo-Fijian sport'. This perception is due to the sport's history and the creation of suggested 'racial myths and narratives of ethnocentrism' that depict Indo-Fijians as unable and ill equipped for rugby participation and leadership (Prasad, 2013, p. 25). Off the field, soccer's organisation stands in opposition to the FRU in its Indo-Fijian make-up. Formerly known as the Fijian Indian Football Association – and now just the Fijian Football Association (FFA) – the FFA began life as a racial organisation and a rare assembly for Indo-Fijians who had been sidelined from the official corridors of state power (Prasad, 2013). Today, participation in soccer is relatively mixed, and at the elite level, there are even more Indigenous players than Indo-Fijians. Yet in terms of leadership, the FFA – along with the majority of coaches and administration staff around the islands – are Indo-Fijian. As such, Indigenous ex-players have been complaining about a lack of access to leadership positions (see Sugden, 2017).

There is little evidence that the FRU is actively seeking to engage the sizeable Indo-Fijian community, in part due to the widespread perception that Indo-Fijians lack physical acumen. This means that there are significant barriers for Indo-Fijian rugby players and coaches who wish to engage with rugby. The FFA, on the other hand, is more inclusive in its outlook.

Continued

Yet their approach to management and leadership is nepotistic; those who run the game are almost exclusively of Indo-Fijian ethnicity, whether by custom or design. Indeed, the absence from the FFA administration of former Indo-Fijian soccer players is something to which the latter object, though this has had no impact on Fiji's soccer hierarchy (Sugden, 2017). It seems that the ethnic barriers to Fijian rugby and soccer are an example of leadership gone wrong – with no partnerships between sports and across ethnic groups, sport in Fiji adds to the barriers to respectful coexistence and integration.

The previous case study highlights the struggles of sport leaders to operate across a web of sporting, sociocultural, ethnic, and generational borders. In the Fijian case, a vicious circle is in place where group identities and sport participation affect each other, and where the separation of groups goes hand in hand with the creation and establishment of borders between sports.

In contrast to Fiji, a football association from a neighbouring Pacific Island region has set the benchmark for crossing sporting borders in an attempt to achieve wider community sport and health benefits. The Cook Islands Football Association's *Just Play* programme – an SFD initiative aimed at sport participation, social development, gender equity, and health promotion – has started to collaborate strategically with other sporting bodies on the island to leverage their programmes through festivals and events (see www.justplay.org; Schulenkorf, 2016). Here, the local *Just Play* development officer used her combined personal, social, cultural, and business literacy to make a difference; in short, she took leadership and decided to embrace cross-sport cooperation to maximise community benefits. In doing so, she built on existing strengths of other sport federations in the country, especially high-profile (and well-resourced) sports such as Rugby and Netball. The so-called *Just Play* Festivals thus benefit from the support and collaboration of different sporting codes, thereby providing an opportunity to play sports together, explore new sports, and develop skills and techniques. More importantly, they also allow for social, cultural, and educational engagement through linked activities. In other words, the leaders saw the festivals as an opportunity to create awareness and engagement across the board and they achieved buy-in and support from key partners, including the Ministry of Education, Ministry of Sport, Ministry of Health, the local police, the Red Cross, and so on. All these institutions provide in-kind support in an attempt to communicate social and health-related messages to children and their families. For instance, the police conduct workshops on crime prevention, while the Red Cross provides first aid and health awareness sessions for families. As such, the festivals live up to their overall goal of achieving both sport-specific and non-sport development outcomes.

The leadership of the *Just Play* development officer was crucial in establishing cross-sport and cross-industry collaborations. Her status in the community, her talent to engage and convince others, and her ability and openness to 'turn vision into reality' resulted in fruitful and ongoing relationships between local stakeholders. Referring back to the working definition provided at the beginning of this chapter, she was able to establish cross-border leadership through *an inclusive and dynamic process of listening, learning, challenging, influencing, guiding, and motivating others across diverse contexts and backgrounds with the intent of leading them towards a relevant, meaningful, and coherent goal.*

Conclusion

This chapter set out to explore the phenomenon of leadership across borders. We started by defining cross-border leadership as an inclusive and dynamic process of listening, learning, challenging, influencing, guiding, and motivating others across diverse contexts and backgrounds with the intent of leading them towards a relevant, meaningful, and coherent goal. Building on this working definition, we outlined key traits and competencies of cross-border leaders and discussed managerial challenges related to sport leadership across geographical, sociocultural, generational, and sporting borders. In doing so, we referred to current research in international settings, including a cross-border case study from Fiji that illustrated the complex nature of leadership across sporting and sociocultural divides.

Leadership across borders presents a challenging yet fascinating space; in short, it requires not only universal leadership characteristics but also culturally contingent ones (Dickson, Castano, Magomaeva, & Den Hartog, 2012). While universal characteristics are phenomena or motivations possessed by people regardless of cultural differences, including charisma, providing work satisfaction and motivation to followers, being dynamic, having good communication skills, and having foresight or vision, culturally contingent characteristics are context-specific and therefore valued differently between groups. They include aspects such as risk-taking, ambition, self-sacrifice, sincerity, sensitivity, wilfulness, compassion, and enthusiasm. A combination of these two fields will allow inclusive cross-border leaders to tackle challenges 'glocally' – an approach that to date only very few champions have successfully employed in the sporting world.

Overall, the ability of leaders to inspire others remains of central importance. In fact, it has been suggested that part of what defines a good cross-border leader also defines a good leader in general – someone who can "turn vision into reality" (Alon & Higgens, 2005). This holds true for any leadership engagement across geographical, sociocultural, political, generational, and sporting borders. To have any chance of turning vision into reality, cross-border leaders have to ensure that power dynamics are balanced, that there is equity in decision-making, and that (local and international) knowledges are respected. In short, cross-border leaders navigate a multifaceted and far from straightforward space in which they must aim to achieve relevant, meaningful, and coherent goals.

References

Adriaanse, J. (2017). Gender diversity in the governance of international sport federations. In N. Schulenkorf & S. Frawley (Eds.), *Critical issues in global sport management* (pp. 23–37). Abingdon: Routledge.

Alon, I., & Higgins, J. M. (2005). Global leadership success through emotional and cultural intelligences. *Business Horizons, 48,* 501–512.

Barnlund, D. C., & Araki, S. (1985). Intercultural encounters: The management of compliments by Japanese and Americans. *Journal of Cross-Cultural Psychology, 16*(1), 9–26. doi:10.1177/0022002185016001002

Bird, A., & Mendenhall, M. E. (2016). From cross-cultural management to global leadership: Evolution and adaption. *Journal of World Business, 51,* 115–126.

Caligiuri, P., & Tarique, I. (2009). Predicting effectiveness in global leadership activities. *Journal of World Business, 44,* 336–346.

Coalter, F. (2010). The politics of sport-for-development: Limited focus programmes and broad gauge problems? *International Review for the Sociology of Sport, 45*(3), 295–314. doi:10.1177/1012690210366791

Cohen, A., & Welty Peachey, J. (2015). The making of a social entrepreneur: From participant to cause champion within a sport-for-development context. *Sport Management Review, 18*(1), 111–125. doi:10.1016/j.smr.2014.04.002

Commeh, M. K., & Schulenkorf, N. (2008). Brenu beach resort, Ghana. In J. Carlsen, J. Liburd, D. Edwards, & P. Forde (Eds.), *Innovation for sustainable tourism: International case studies* (pp. 76–84). Esbjerg, Denmark: BEST Education Network.

Cruickshank, A., & Collins, D. (2016). Advancing leadership in sport: Time to take off the blinkers? *Sports Medicine, 46,* 1199–1204.

Dickson, M. W., Castano, N., Magomaeva, A., & Den Hartog, D. N. (2012). Conceptualising leadership across cultures. *Journal of World Business, 47,* 483–492.

Fiji Bureau of Statistics. (2015). *Population and labour force estimates of 2014.* (Statistical Report No. 99). Suva: Fiji Government.

Guinness, D., & Besnier, N. (2016). Nation, nationalism, and sport: Fijian rugby in the Local–Global nexus. *Anthropological Quarterly, 89*(4), 1109–1141.

Jokinen, T. (2005). Global leadership competencies: A review and discussion. *Journal of European Industrial Training, 29*(3), 199–216.

Lal, B. (2012). Editorial: Fiji's coup conundrum. *The Round Table, 101*(6), 489–497.

Lindsey, I., & Grattan, A. (2012). An 'International Movement'? Decentring sport-for-development within Zambian communities. *International Journal of Sport Policy and Politics, 4*(1), 91–110.

McCall, M. W., Jr., & Hollenbeck, G. P. (2002). *Developing global executives: The lessons of international experience.* Boston, MA: Harvard Business School Press.

Mendenhall, M. E., Reiche, B. S., Bird, A., & Osland, J. S. (2012). Defining the 'Global' in global leadership. *Journal of World Business, 47,* 493–503.

Miraftab, F. (1997). Flirting with the enemy: Challenges faced by NGOs in development and empowerment. *Habitat International, 21*(4), 361–375. doi:10.1016/S0197-3975(97)00011-8

Prasad, M. (2013). Sidelines and solidarity: Race and cultural hegemonies in the transition from mission to national soccer in Fiji and South Africa. *The Journal of Pacific Studies, 33*(1), 26–43.

Presterudstuen, G. H. (2010). The mimicry of men: Rugby and masculinities in postcolonial Fiji. *The Global Studies Journal, 3*(2), 237–247.

Presterudstuen, G. H. (2016). Performing masculinity through Christian devotion: Methodism, manhood and colonial mimicry in Fiji. *Interventions, 18*(1), 107–126.

Presterudstuen, G. H., & Schieder, D. (2016). Bati as bodily labour: Rethinking masculinity and violence in Fiji. *The Asia Pacific Journal of Anthropology, 17*(3–4), 213–230.

Richards, J., Kaufman, Z., Schulenkorf, N., Wolff, E., Gannett, K., Siefken, K., & Rodriguez, G. (2013). Advancing the evidence base of sport for development: A new open-access, peer-reviewed journal. *Journal of Sport for Development, 1*(1), 1–3.

Robertson, R. (2012). Cooking the goose: Fiji's coup culture contextualised. *The Round Table, 101*(6), 509–519.

Rockstuhl, T., Seiler, S., Ang, S., Van Dyne, L., & Annen, H. (2011). Beyond general intelligence (IQ) and emotional intelligence (EQ): The role of cultural intelligence (CQ) on cross-border leadership effectiveness in a globalized world. *Journal of Social Issues, 67*(4), 825–840.

Rosen, R., & Digh, P. (2001). Developing globally literate leaders. *Training and Development-Alexandria-American Society for Training and Development, 55*(5), 70–80.

Sato, K., Yuki, M., & Norasakkunkit, V. (2014). A socio-ecological approach to cross-cultural differences in the sensitivity to social rejection: The partially mediating role of relational mobility. *Journal of Cross-Cultural Psychology, 45*(10), 1549–1560. doi:10.1177/0022022114544320

Schulenkorf, N. (2012). Sustainable community development through sport and events: A conceptual framework for sport-for-development projects. *Sport Management Review, 15*(1), 1–12. doi:10.1016/j.smr.2011.06.001

Schulenkorf, N. (2016). The contributions of special events to sport-for-development programs. *Journal of Sport Management, 30*(6), 629–642. doi:10.1123/JSM.2016-0066

Schulenkorf, N., Sherry, E., & Rowe, K. (2016). Sport-for-development: An integrated literature review. *Journal of Sport Management, 30*(1), 22–39. doi:10.1123/jsm.2014-0263

Schulenkorf, N., & Siefken, K. (2019). Managing sport-for-development and healthy lifestyles: The sport-for-health model. *Sport Management Review, 22*(1), 96–107. doi:10.1016/j.smr.2018.09.003

Sherry, E., & Schulenkorf, N. (2016). League Bilong Laif: Rugby, education and sport-for-development partnerships in Papua New Guinea. *Sport, Education and Society, 21*(4), 513–530. doi:10.1080/13573322.2015.1112780

Sherry, E., Schulenkorf, N., & Chalip, L. (2015). Managing sport for social change: The state of play. *Sport Management Review, 18*(1), 1–5. doi:10.1016/j.smr.2014.12.001

Sugden, J. (2006). Teaching and playing sport for conflict resolution and co-existence in Israel. *International Review for the Sociology of Sport, 41*(2), 221–240. doi:10.1177/1012690206075422

Sugden, J. (2017). *Sport and integration: An exploration of group identity and intergroup relations in Fiji.* (PhD Thesis), University of Technology Sydney, Sydney.

Welty Peachey, J., Cohen, A., Shin, N., & Fusaro, B. (2018). Challenges and strategies of building and sustaining inter-organizational partnerships in sport for development and peace. *Sport Management Review, 21*(2), 160–175. doi:10.1016/j.smr.2017.06.002

Welty Peachey, J., Zhou, Y., Damon, Z. J., & Burton, L. J. (2015). Forty years of leadership research in sport management: A review, synthesis, and conceptual framework. *Journal of Sport Management, 29*(5), 570–587. doi:10.1123/jsm.2014-0126

Youseff, C. M., & Lutham, F. (2012). Positive global leadership. *Journal of World Business, 47*, 539–547.

5   Leadership and mega-events

Introduction

Mega-events have become a sought-after urban spectacle for many cities around the world seeking to develop, revitalise, and reinvigorate urban spaces in terms of economic, tourism, and social development. As described by McGillivray and McPherson (2012), cities have become the principal economic agent involved in increasingly inter-urban competition where mega-events serve as an important public policy tool to attract mobile capital, affluent residents, and tourists. The engagement in this competitive strategy comes with significant public policy challenges that cross administrative boundaries, engaging local and state actors, international sport federations, the private sector, and event sanctioning bodies. In cities that use events in a strategic entrepreneurial way, there are drivers of economic growth that come in the form of urban development groups such as coalitions or regimes (Misener & Mason, 2008, 2009).

These groups provide leadership from a civic development perspective and liaise with stakeholders who plan, develop, and implement the actual event. Thus, to speak about leadership around mega-events requires a multiple stakeholder perspective to consider when and where the leadership is coming from based on the aspect of the event. Events of this size and scale also require considerations around the type of leadership needed for the various aspects and the stage of the events process. The event has many stages that often require different skill sets that may not be attainable for one individual or group. In fact, most mega-events have different leaders involved at various stages. There are often leaders involved in the bid stage of the mega-event who are replaced when the organising committee coalesces around the management of the Games. It is necessary to consider all these aspects in considering what types of leaders and what leadership skills are necessary for each situation.

In this chapter, the focus is on two levels of mega-event leadership: (1) urban development coalitions as drivers of the event's agenda and (2) organising committee leadership around the implementation of the actual event. In order to discuss these two perspectives, we draw upon multiple theoretical approaches to consider the stage of the event, the aspects of event management, ownership, partnerships, and impact/legacies of events. Each of these aspects of the event can require different types of leaders based on the demands of the constituents and necessities of the event. Perhaps in the changing economy of events where cities have become more sceptical of hosting gigantic spectacles such as the Olympic and Paralympic Games, leadership is all the more important on multiple levels. As Parent, Olver, and Séguin (2009) articulated, different stages of events and various aspects of the organising process require different types of leaders to take on the roles of guiding the processes.

In fact, Parent et al. (2009) argue that while forms of leadership such as charismatic and transformational were relevant, the multi-linkage model of leadership (Yukl, 1971) was the most meaningful for considering all leadership processes of events. This is not surprising given the multitude of functions, considerations, developments, and political affiliations of such gigantic spectacles. Thus, there is not one singular theoretical perspective that drives the discussion of leaders for mega-events. As articulated throughout this chapter, the leaders in each aspect of the event organising structure are vital to determining the desired outcomes. As Masterman and Wood (2006) has described, the event planning process can be subdivided into ten different stages from the initial discussions and feasibility stages through to the evaluation and feedback stages. However, for the purpose of this chapter, we break down the event process into macro level stages to consider leadership from each perspective: (1) Bid, (2) Planning and Execution, (3) Legacy Planning, and (4) Post-Event.

Bid stage

Mega-events are short-term, high-profile events like the Olympic Games and Football World Cup that have a significant impact on urban and regional environments. As Hiller (2000) has articulated, mega-events have the potential to reprioritise urban agendas, fuel debates about resources priorities, stimulate urban (re)development whether needed or not, and become strong instruments of 'boosterist' ideologies promoting economic growth over social development agendas. In recent years, there has been much critique of the use of events to support pro-growth strategies aimed primarily at economic outcomes (e.g. Black & Westhuizen, 2004; Cashman, Toohey, Darcy, Symons, & Stewart, 2006; Groothuis & Rotthoff, 2016; Nichols & Ralston, 2014; Tolzmann, 2014). Further, there are also some scholars that have begun to consider the ways in which events are used as soft power strategies to alter global perceptions about the image of countries and regions (Grix, 2012; Grix & Houlihan, 2014).

All this positioning speaks to a need for leadership to secure a sport mega-event for a city/region. It is not simply about an individual with the requisite skills but, rather, groups of stakeholders with the political and economic capacity to convince the local population that hosting such a large-scale event is a worthy and viable option. This requires a particular type of urban political leader to galvanise an agenda. Such a leader is typically different from the organising committee leader. For example, for the Toronto 2015 PanAm/Parapan American Games, David Peterson, former Premier of the Province of Ontario led the bid.

It should also be noted that he replaced the original leader of the bid, Roger Garland, who stepped down for unknown reasons during the bid process. In both cases, their political leadership skills were crucial to the process.

Given that bids are led mainly by personnel from the city and region, driving a particular development or growth agenda, it is logical that some level of civic structure is in place to facilitate the leadership role. Misener and Mason (2008, 2009) have argued that where mega-events are pursued as part of a political and economic agenda, governing coalitions often known as 'urban regimes' can serve a key leadership role. Urban regimes, as defined by Stone (1989), represent "the informal arrangements by which public bodies and private interests function together in order to be able to make and carry out governing decisions" (p. 6). He further argued that the opportunity presented enables urban political leadership to forge alliances with resourceful societal actors, primarily the corporate sector, to support development initiatives such as mega-events. While some, such as Lawless (1994), have rejected the idea of urban regimes in non-United States cities because of differing political ideologies, the theory has proved useful in numerous international contexts in understanding how and why institutions become involved in interorganisational partnerships around particular development agendas. Regime theory is an American neo-pluralist account of urban politics that is typically concerned with local collaborative dynamics and processes, particularly those between local government and business leaders. This approach has proven useful in the past in understanding how and why cities support mega-events as part of the urban development agendas.

The reformulation of regime theory as provided by Stoker and Mossberger (1994) represents an important acknowledgement of culture and ideology in shaping regime character and, importantly, the role of key local leaders in supporting the regime agenda. The reason why this perspective is so important in considering the bid stage of the mega-event process is that political and corporate leaders can shift over the duration of the bid and the event, but the urban regime persists around a central development ideology. Hence, the regime itself plays a critical role in strategically leading the process. These urban elites thus form the key leadership group in the initial processes of bid and development stages. As Misener and Mason (2010) have pointed out, those cities with an enduring urban regime have also been some of the most successful cities in bidding for and securing events aligned with an entrepreneurial development agenda (e.g. Melbourne, Australia). In each of the cases Misener and Mason examined, they were able to demonstrate the importance of key leaders in the city, such as mayors, corporate executives, sporting champions, sporting administrators, and others, in supporting the work of the regimes in their work guiding the events process. The regimes were essential in supporting the ideas behind the bid for a mega-event and instrumental in clearly aligning the strategic initiatives of events to the city, region, and national development agenda. It is only with this kind of civic leadership that a bid can truly be successful, especially in the context of urban development agendas.

Competition among cities for private investment in the mega-events processes has become a powerful incentive for the political leadership to embark on a collaborative strategy with the corporate sector to secure investments and resources to boost local economies. These urban governance arrangements are embedded in institutional frameworks that define their scope of action and provide opportunity structures for urban political action when the appropriate leadership is in place to drive this agenda. Relatedly, theories of urban governance emphasise the constraints on political and institutional control with a need to consider the importance of societal involvement to achieve collective goals (Jessop, 2002). This is most apparent in the way that political leaders frame the economic, social, and tourism opportunities of hosting an event to seek consent and support, which is typically achieved through referenda or plebiscites (Hiller & Wanner, 2011). However, in this context, it must be acknowledged that cities are a web of complex contingencies with relationships with regions, central government, and transnational institutions, such as the EU, as well as associations with private business sectors (Pierre, 2014). It is the role of the leadership teams to catalyse the necessary support for a bid to be successful. There are numerous challenges and power struggles within this process that tend to marginalise the interests of those with less power. Leaders herein must have the character and political shrewdness to navigate this challenging terrain.

Further to the urban governing groups, the bid process involves a committee, which is often made up of key players from the regime and others from sectors with high levels of influence in economic and political landscapes. A key part of the process at this stage is securing a leader for the bid that has political savvy as well as the community-mindedness to demonstrate the value of hosting a mega-event. As Parent et al. (2009) demonstrated, at this stage it is important to have a charismatic and/or transformational leader who can galvanise the public around the goodwill brought about by hosting such a large-scale economic project. Given the aforementioned discussion of the intertwining of urban politics with event processes, the importance of political leadership cannot be understated at this stage. The need to secure financial commitments from public and private sectors, along with securing corporate support for the costs associated with hosting the Games is crucial. Thus, at this stage it is really about the transformational character and abilities of a leader capable of stimulating support. It is common to see a different person leading the bid stage than will ultimately be leading the organising committee as the process moves into the stage of development. An example of this leadership scenario is Lord Sebastien Coe and his leadership of the London 2012 Summer Olympic and Paralympic Games. Coe took over the leadership role after Barbara Cassini, a prominent American businesswoman, stepped down. She reportedly felt that Coe had the charismatic leadership necessary to secure the 2012 Games. In the lead up to the decision, London was considered second to Paris during the bid process; however, Coe's inspirational speech during the evaluation meetings is reported to have changed the tide in favour of London, which ultimately secured the Games

(Lee, Warner, & Bond, 2006). This example demonstrates the important role of a charismatic or transformational leader at that time in the process.

Planning phase

There has been a significant increase in the professionalisation of event management over the past three decades, and the realm of mega-events has been part of this change. Event management has emerged as a prominent profession and an important part of university programmes globally (Goldblatt, 2004). This has also led to a rise in the number of professionals involved in events and those seeking to lead the large-scale event organisations. Typically, an organising committee for a mega-event such as the Olympic and Paralympic Games has a temporary workforce consisting of 3,000–5,000 employees for a Winter Games and up to 20,000 for a Summer Games (Van der Wagen, 2007). Mega-events can have upwards of 50 functional areas or divisions to set forth the necessary tasks of the committee. A seven- to ten-year planning time frame requires a level of organisational skill and capacity to oversee all of the necessary aspects of planning and implementation. However, planning is not the only aspect of leadership in this stage. The ongoing relationship management with political supporters and dissidents, liaison with corporate partners, and ultimately being the public face of the Games management are critical functions. This is an extensive skill set and requires a leader to be adaptable, flexible, politically savvy, and of strong character. Parent and Smith-Swan (2013) described a ten-stage process of human resource management surrounding an event, which started with the initial stage of hiring the leader. The leader is responsible for ensuring the following nine stages of the event management are completed: business plan, organisational structure, human resources plan, human resources policies and procedures, workforce recruitment and training, supervision of workforce, post-Games workforce plans, and the event wrap-up. Within all of these stages the leader is also responsible for navigating and managing various stakeholder interests and expectations.

As Parent et al. (2009) described in their case study of the 2005 Fédération Internationale de Natation (FINA) World Aquatics Championships there is potential for different styles of leadership to be necessary depending on the nature of the event. In the case of the FINA World Championships, they determined that while charismatic and transformational leadership traits were relevant for an event at risk of failing, ultimately, they decided that the multiple linkage model was most appropriate for considering organising committee leadership. The multiple linkage model of leadership put forth by Yukl (1971) suggests that the impact of leader behaviours is complex and based on four specific variables: (1) managerial behaviours, (2) intervening variables, (3) criterion variables, and (4) situational variables. The challenge with this model is its complexity, and to date sport or event management researchers have not adopted the approach. However, the complexity of the model reflects the complexity of mega-event leadership and the unique situations and challenges they present. This theory supports the idea that taking into account the behaviours of the leaders in relation to the situational variables such as culture, political climate, and task urgency. Situational variables can moderate leader behaviours in relation to the criterion variables of what is required of the specific roles and responsibilities. This also requires consideration of the intervening variables of task commitment, role ability and clarity, work organisation, cooperation and trust, resources and support, and external coordination requirements. Each is key to considering the various characteristics of event processes and how different tasks are related to the environmental, political, and cultural challenges faced by leaders.

It is important to consider that managing mega-events does involve leadership across multiple levels. Certainly, the individual chosen to the be the CEO of the organising committee sets the tenor in terms of addressing the variables associated with managing the mega-event and the implementation of broader strategy. An important aspect when considering leadership from the perspective of an organising committee is the multiplicity of stakeholders involved in the event delivery. Parent (2008) and Parent and Séguin (2007) have demonstrated the importance of considering and understanding the various stakeholders and their event agendas and activities. Leaders must therefore understand how stakeholders can influence the staging of an event, given that the relationship with stakeholders and the leader can influence "communication, information exchange, resource acquisition, organisational identity formation, and various other organisational actions" (Parent & Séguin, 2007, p. 90). Ultimately, as Emery (2010) has pointed out, the success of managing mega-event stakeholders depends upon the effective and efficient management of the tripartite relationship of sport, media, and the event funders.

Test events in the lead up to the main event can serve an important role in ironing out any of the challenges associated with stakeholders and the event operations (Andersen, Hanstad, & Plejdrup-Skillestad, 2015). It is also an important opportunity for leaders have the chance to consider any needed course redirections without the same level of media attention that is paid to the larger event. This serves a crucial role for leaders who are put in the spotlight for the duration of the event, regardless of their actual role in the actual organisational processes on the ground of the event.

A key issue that has arisen around some international sport events has been the change in leadership throughout the event planning process. As alluded to earlier the study by Parent et al. (2009) of the FINA World Aquatic Championships is a good example of the challenges event leaders can face during their tenure. In that case, the city faced significant challenges in event preparations, effectively cancelling the event, only to have the event returned to the city under a different leadership group. Essentially, there were two different leaders with contrasting approaches and objectives. The second organising committee had a very different outwardly focussed role when managing the image created by a 'failed' attempt to host, but also a time-sensitive management role to ensure a successful event. In that case, the leader was the city mayor, who offered a politically savvy style when dealing with corporate and political stakeholders, but the management team also knew how to get the job done. This is a managerial role in many ways, but it also demonstrates the need for the leader to be able to support and enable leadership from within the organisation to carry out the business plan.

For the Toronto 2015 PanAm/Parapan American Games, there was a change in leadership during the course of planning the event. Ian Troop, CEO of the organising committee, was allegedly fired from the role due to 'leadership issues' and operational challenges 18 months out from the start of the Games. It was revealed in the media that there were economic challenges and questions regarding salaries and spending by the leadership. While there were no confirmed reports of the leader leaving due to economic challenges, it certainly sheds light on the role of the leader and the need to ensure strong character and integrity. In this case, the leadership change happened and the final stages of planning and the implementation of the event took place under new leadership. As part of the change in leadership, a media liaison was also brought in to deal directly with the media and manage issues and crises as they arose. Around the same time as the new leader. This media liaison was renowned for dealing with media around political scandals and leadership changes, which speaks to the needs in that particular role in time of a potentially tumultuous and politically charged change. What is also noteworthy, though, is that functional area planning continued to run relatively smoothly because the previous CEO had developed a group of strong leaders in each of the event's functional areas to ensure solid preparations for the event.

Another noteworthy example early in the planning process of the Toronto 2015 PanAm/Parapan American Games involved leaders of the Board deciding that it was vital to ensure the strength of leadership with the Parasport aspects of the Games. In order to do so, they recruited a Senior Manager of Parapan Integration who had previously worked on the Vancouver 2010 Paralympic Games. The aim of this role was to take ownership of and responsibility for full integration of Parasport for the whole Games. This decision on the part of the leadership team, to create a senior management position for the role, was a demonstration of a commitment to fully integrating Parasports.

As highlighted in these examples, the concept of leader character emerges as an important concept. If a leader of a mega-event fails to show the necessary character to lead, then they are unlikely to gain the support of the workforce or the general community. As Crossan, Seijts, and Gandz (2015) have articulated, character is fundamental to leadership, particularly in complex organisations. Character sets the tone for how people engage with others around them and demonstrates the importance of behaviours and activities that support the values and virtues of an organisation. While there is no agreed-upon definition of character, scholars have tended to emphasise the personality traits, values, and virtues which support the mission and vision of an organisation. These ideas are discussed more fully in the chapter on diversity and leadership but are worth noting here because of the importance of character as a factor for effective decision-making. In the case where leaders make poor decisions that can negatively impact their organisation, as has been demonstrated in a number of mega-events, the consequence for the event, the city, and the nation can be dire.

Legacy planning

While planning for positive outcomes when hosting sport mega-events is not necessarily divorced from the broader event planning and execution process, we offer this as a distinct realm of leadership to demonstrate its importance especially over the past two decades. Furthermore, many mega-events have begun to adopt a model where the legacy planning is distinct or separate from the planning for the actual event (Harris & Houlihan, 2016; Weiler, 2011). The concept of legacy has become a major part of the sport event lexicon as an attempt to address the negative economic, social, and environmental consequences that mega-events often generate for host cities. Legacy is used in a primarily positive manner to refer to the so-called positive outcomes of hosting an event in the city, often framing anything and everything of the leftovers from the event (Preuss, 2007, 2015). Some scholars have argued for the need to consider legacy in a more timebound and geographically sensitive way to capture the essence of these leftover assets, such as infrastructure, volunteers, social capital, sport participation, and tourism, to name a few (Dickson, Benson, & Blackman, 2011). One question remains in the scholarly literature around event legacies: who is responsible for enabling legacy? Some have argued that the organising committee cannot be the locus of responsibility for legacy because this group is too focussed on organising the actual event to be focussed on the resultant outcomes (Girginov & Hills, 2008; Kassens-Noor, Wilson, Müller, Maharaj, & Huntoon, 2015). Hence, it is essential to have strong leadership as part of the legacy planning to ensure that desired outcomes are achieved. In the face of adverse economic and political situations, it is these components of the mega-event that will be pushed aside in the face of Games delivery, and therefore the event requires a leader who is both community oriented and politically astute to navigate the challenges of implementing the event legacy plans.

Two different examples of leadership models enabling collaboration for legacy will be highlighted here. The important detail in each situation is that responsibility is removed from the organising committee and the appointed legacy leaders assume control over legacy plans and strategy, aligning them with the broader Games objectives. In the first scenario, the Vancouver 2010 Olympic and Paralympic Games Organising Committee established a parallel organisation known as Legacies Now 2010. In an International Olympic Committee (IOC) commissioned report, Weiler and Mohan (2009) discussed how the Vancouver-Whistler Bid Committee and the government of British Columbia sought to gain support early on for the bid and made a commitment to investing and building capacity in the sport system. This led to the creation of Legacies Now by the bid corporation that then followed on through once Vancouver were awarded the Games. Legacies Now functioned alongside the organising committee as a separate entity that had representation from a number of sectors including tourism, community development, accessibility, and inclusion. While not an official partner of Vancouver Organising Committee for the 2010 Olympic and Paralympic Winter Games (VANOC), they were involved in partner meetings, and many of the staff members of Legacies Now were members of VANOC committees. The organisation functioned as a separate entity focussing on three legacy areas: sport development, community capacity building, and a province-wide community outreach programme. Essentially, the organisation as a whole serves to demonstrate the important leadership role in focussing on and securing a legacy for a mega-event such as the Olympic and Paralympic Games. In this case, the decision to have Bruce Dewar lead Legacies Now from the early stages to post-Games is indicative of the importance of leadership character. Coming from a background in tourism and business sustainability consulting, he was able to catalyse the efforts around innovative, entrepreneurial, and socially responsible activities for the organisation that resulted in a number of very successful social programmes. In addition, post-Games Bruce Dewar has led the evolution of Legacies Now to its current philanthropic organisation: LIFT Philanthropy. LIFT provides financial and business skills support for social purpose organisations to succeed in getting the tools necessary to support underserved and marginalised populations. This leadership approach is unparalleled in previous models of Olympic and Paralympic Games organising.

In a similar approach, the Toronto 2015 Parapan American Games held in Toronto sought to develop a similar strategy to build on the momentum of these Games for the disability sport community. In this case, the organising committee TO2015 had its own legacy agenda that was embedded in the Games strategy. But others in the disability sport community saw the Parapan Games as an opportunity to capitalise on the event to create more sport opportunities for Ontarians with disabilities. In order to make that happen, there needed to be a different organisational structure that coordinated these efforts. It was under the leadership of Karen O'Neill, CEO of the Canadian Paralympic Committee (CPC), that this structure was enabled (see insert for a profile of Karen O'Neill). She saw the event and the policy imperative of the Accessibility for Ontarians with Disabilities Act to leverage existing programmes within the CPC, and to use the opportunity of the Toronto 2015 Parapan American Games to focus on partnerships and sport system alignment in the Province of Ontario. The Ontario Parasport Legacy Group (OPLG) was born out of a provincial summit that culminated in unanimous support for a leadership group to focus on leveraging the Games. While O'Neill was a driving force behind the creation of this group and played a key role throughout the leveraging process, the Legacy Group functioned on a model of collective shared leadership. Pearce and Conger (2003) determined that shared leadership is a dynamic and interactive process among people in a group for which the objective is to achieve a shared goal. In this situation, leadership is broadly distributed instead of being centralised with one individual. Contractor, DeChurch, Carson, Carter, and Keegan (2012) have further described this group functioning as configurations in a social network where each actor plays a key leadership role at a particular point in the network. This approach describes the functioning of the OPLG, where individuals within the group have shared responsibility for achieving the goals, securing resources, and contributing to the overall success. It was an opportunity for many to get involved in the delivery of a Games-related legacy and enhance the offerings of their own organisations. This group evolved into the Ontario Parasport Collective post-Games and has been critical in moving towards a more aligned system of Parasport development in the province. In fact, given the integration between sport, recreation, health, and educational institutions, it is likely to become a model to examine for future host cities seeking to maximise Games legacies.

Regardless of the approach taken in developing a legacy and positive social outcomes from a mega-event, this objective is now an imperative of the event process and requires strong leadership to ensure it occurs. The examples provided here indicate that in most situations it is important for legacy planning to be removed from the organising committee level because the leadership in that scenario must focus on delivering the event. Further, there needs to be a model of leadership that provides for continuity post-Games. Legacy planning is not simply about developing strategies before and during the Games but also about having a well-considered legacy plan to be delivered post-event. From this perspective, there will also need to be succession planning in terms of leadership, given the temporal nature of organising committees. The potential enduring leadership variable here is the Legacy Group, while the members of the organising committee will disperse and seek out new opportunities elsewhere, as that organisation will cease to exist shortly after the event.

Post-event

The post mega-event stage is likely the most challenging from a leadership perspective. As described earlier, both the bid committees and the organising committees are temporary organisations that cease to exist post-event (Lowendahl, 1995). Yet there is still much surrounding the event that needs to be accomplished once the event has officially left town. We return to the idea that the urban development coalitions in the host city need to play a key role in ensuring the wrap-up of the event, that post-event legacy plans are in place, and that the handover processes of venues and related assets are completed with accountability and diligence. The other key element – that can all too easily be lost in the process without effective leadership – is the transfer of knowledge (known as the TOK process in mega-event networks). This process will have begun prior to the completion of the event, but it is a critical process in ensuring that the next host city receives the appropriate knowledge and information about the event (Halbwirth & Toohey, 2001). This can include event evaluation, which is typically a key accountability measure, and one that provides valuable knowledge for future hosts. For example, the International Olympic Committee's Olympic Games Knowledge Management programme allows future host cities to benefit from the latest knowledge and experiences gained from their events. Without the requirement embedded, this process is all too easily lost. Thus, clarity of leadership throughout the process is necessary, including the final stages in dis-solving the organising committee and reporting procedures.

Part of the process of the Games is also about measuring and evaluating the event so that knowledge and relevant data can be passed to future organising committees. Thus, a leader throughout the process must be someone who values organisational learning and the research process. It is now up to cities to conduct their own evaluations with the necessary accountability to international governing bodies. Thus, the thought leadership necessary here to push the agenda of research and evaluation is crucial to the overall process. As McGillivray and McPherson (2012) articulated, all too often event host cities/nations are be-holden to international governing bodies and event owners. It is when a leader is armed with the necessary information from previous Games evaluations and knowledge transfer that they can negotiate with event governing bodies for bet-ter conditions, earmark and cap public sector contributions for the benefit of communities and get realistic projections regarding the costs and benefits of hosting mega-events.

Conclusion

In this chapter, we have articulated that there is not one simple leadership strat-egy related to mega-events. In fact, the complexity of a mega-event suggests that there are various strategies associated with different types of events and compli-cations that might arise throughout the process that require different types of leadership skills. Certainly, it cannot be overstated that leaders of mega-events require highly developed political and media skills in today's digital environ-ment. The works of Parent and colleagues (2008, 2009) have pointed to models such as the multiple linkages approach, which considers the complexity of the situation and the many variables associated with a shifting agenda throughout the life cycle of the event. The context of urban development is also critical to considering how events are shaped and driven with the understanding that leadership needs to come from a coalition within the context of the city. The urban development literature offers some perspective when considering leader-ship approaches from the city level (Mason, Sant, & Misener, 2017; Misener & Mason, 2008, 2009) offering insights into the leadership potential of these ur-ban development groups.

At various stages of the event, there needs to be consideration of the unique processes that might require a different approach. Certainly, during the bid phase, there is a great need for political posturing but also the ability to gar-ner wider community support. This is increasingly a central role of the leader in the bid committee. During the planning phase, there are significant managerial functions that a leader needs to be involved in, but also have the capacity to en-able leadership in others who oversee the functional programme of the event. This, of course, all underscores the leader's important work with multiple part-ners from government, public, and private sectors, and in being a conduit to the media. We have argued that legacy planning is a distinct aspect of the events process, and there are some more recent models to consider in terms of leadership around legacy planning. A host city/region needs to decide how to navigate the need to create a positive impact on the local community and what model of leadership and management might work most appropriately. And, finally, the post-event stage is critical and perhaps one area that is severely understudied. What happens to leaders and the leadership once the event has left town? There is ample work to be accomplished immediately following the event, and thus the leader needs to be prepared to continue the evaluation and knowledge transfer on to completion. Thus, there is not one model of leadership that fits well in the mega-events process, but rather it is a conglomeration of multiple approaches and strategies depending on the scenario at hand. Each event is unique, and thus leadership needs to be addressed according to the needs and desires of the particular mega-event.

References

Andersen, S. S., Hanstad, D. V., & Plejdrup-Skillestad, K. (2015). The role of test events in major sporting events. *Event Management, 19*(2), 261–273.

Black, D., & Van Der Westhuizen, J. (2004). The allure of global games for 'semi-peripheral' polities and spaces: a research agenda. *Third World Quarterly, 25*(7), 1195–1214.

Cashman, R., Toohey, K., Darcy, S., Symons, C., & Stewart, B. (2006). When the carnival is over: Evaluating the outcomes of mega-events, by R. Cashman. *Sporting Traditions, 21*(1), 1–32.

Contractor, N. S., DeChurch, L. A., Carson, J., Carter, D. R., & Keegan, B. (2012). The topology of collective leadership. *The Leadership Quarterly, 23*(6), 994–1011. doi:10.1016/J.LEAQUA.2012.10.010

Crossan, M., Seijts, G., & Gandz, J. (2015, December 15). Developing leadership character. *Ivey Business Journal, January/February*, 1–6. doi:10.4324/9781315739809

Dickson, T. J., Benson, A. M., & Blackman, D. A. (2011). Developing a framework for evaluating Olympic and Paralympic legacies. *Journal of Sport & Tourism, 16*(4), 285–302. doi:10.1080/14775085.2011.635014

Emery, P. (2010). Past, present, future major sport event management practice: The practitioner perspective. *Sport Management Review, 13*(2), 158–170. doi:10.1016/J.SMR.2009.06.003

Girginov, V., & Hills, L. (2008). A sustainable sports legacy: Creating a link between the London Olympics and sports participation. *The International Journal of the History of Sport, 25*(14), 2091–2116. doi:10.1080/09523360802439015

Grix, J. (2012). 'Image' leveraging and sports mega-events: Germany and the 2006 FIFA World Cup. *Journal of Sport & Tourism, 17*(4), 289–312. doi:10.1080/14775085.20 12.760934

Grix, J., & Houlihan, B. (2014). Sports mega-events as part of a nation's soft power strategy: The cases of Germany (2006) and the UK (2012). *The British Journal of Politics & International Relations, 16*(4), 572–596. doi:10.1111/1467-856X.12017

Goldblatt, J. J. (2004). *Special events: Event leadership for a new world.* New York: John Wiley & Sons.

Groothuis, P. A., & Rotthoff, K. W. (2016). The economic impact and civic pride effects of sports teams and mega-events: Do the public and the professionals agree? *Economic Affairs, 36*(1), 21–32. doi:10.1111/ecaf.12156

Halbwirth, S., & Toohey, K. (2001). The Olympic Games and knowledge management: A case study of the Sydney organising committee of the Olympic Games. *European Sport Management Quarterly, 1*(2), 91–111.

Harris, S., & Houlihan, B. (2016). Implementing the community sport legacy: The limits of partnerships, contracts and performance management. *European Sport Management Quarterly, 16*(4), 433–458. doi:10.1080/16184742.2016.1178315

Hiller, H. H. (2000). Mega-events, urban boosterism and growth strategies: An analysis of the objectives and legitimations of the Cape Town 2004 Olympic bid. *International Journal of Urban and Regional Research, 24*(2), 439–458. doi:10.1111/1468-2427.00256

Hiller, H. H., & Wanner, R. A. (2011). Public opinion in host Olympic cities: The case of the 2010 Vancouver Winter Games. *Sociology, 45*(5), 883–899.

Jessop, B. (2002). Liberalism, neoliberalism, and urban governance: A state–theoretical perspective. *Antipode, 34*(3), 452–472.

Kassens-Noor, E., Wilson, M., Müller, S., Maharaj, B., & Huntoon, L. (2015). Towards a mega-event legacy framework. *Leisure Studies, 34*(6). doi:10.1080/02614367.2015.1035316

Lee, M., Warner, A., & Bond, D. (2006). *The race for the 2012 Olympics: The inside story on how London won the bid*. London: Virgin Books.

Lowendahl, B. R. (1995). Organizing the Lillehammer Olympic Winter Games. *Scandinavian Journal of Management, 11*(4), 347–362.

Mason, D., Sant, S.-L., & Misener, L. (2017). Leveraging sport and entertainment facilities in small- to mid-sized cities. *Marketing Intelligence and Planning*. doi:10.1108/MIP-04-2017-0065

Masterman, G., & Wood, E. H. (2006). *Innovative marketing communications: Strategies for the events industry*. London: Routledge.

Mcgillivray, D., & Mcpherson, G. (2012). Mega events : Neoliberalized vehicle or opportunity for strategic global leadership. *Journal of Leadership, Accountability and Ethics, 9*(5), 80–92.

Misener, L., & Mason, D. S. (2008). Urban regimes and the sporting events agenda: A cross national comparison of civic development strategies. *Journal of Sport Management, 22*, 603–627.

Misener, L., & Mason, D. S. (2009). Fostering community development through sporting events strategies: An examination of urban regime perceptions. *Journal of Sport Management, 23*(6), 770–794.

Misener, L., & Mason, D. (2010). Towards a community centred approach to corporate community involvement in the sporting events agenda. *Journal of Management & Organization, 16*(4), 495–514.

Nichols, G., & Ralston, R. (2014). The legacy costs of delivering the 2012 Olympic and Paralympic Games through regulatory capitalism. *Leisure Studies*, (December 2014), 1–16. doi:10.1080/02614367.2014.923495

Parent, M., & Smith-Swan, S. (2013). *Managing major sports events: Theory and practice*. New York: Routledge.

Parent, M. M. (2008). Evolution and issue patterns for major-sport-event organizing committees and their stakeholders. *Journal of Sport Management, 22*(2), 135–164. doi:10.1123/jsm.22.2.135

Parent, M. M., Olver, D., & Séguin, B. (2009). Understanding leadership in major sporting events: The case of the 2005 world aquatics championships. *Sport Management Review, 12*(3), 167–184. doi:10.1016/J.SMR.2009.01.004

Parent, M. M., & Séguin, B. (2007). Factors that led to the drowning of a world championship organizing committee: A stakeholder approach. *European Sport Management Quarterly, 7*(2), 187–212. doi:10.1080/16184740701353372

Pearce, C. L., & Conger, J. A. (Eds.). (2003). *Shared leadership: Reframing the hows and whys of leadership.* Thousand Oaks, CA: Sage Publications.

Pierre, J. (2014). Can urban regimes travel in time and space? Urban regime theory, urban governance theory, and comparative urban politics. *Urban Affairs Review, 50*(6), 864–889. doi:10.1177/1078087413518175

Preuss, H. (2007). The conceptualisation and measurement of mega sport event legacies. *Journal of Sport & Tourism, 12*(3), 207–228.

Preuss, H. (2015). A framework for identifying the legacies of a mega sport event. *Leisure Studies,* 37–41. doi:10.1080/02614367.2014.994552

Stoker, G., & Mossberger, K. (1994). Urban regime theory in comparative perspective. *Environment and Planning C: Government and Policy, 12*(2), 195–212.

Tolzmann, M. C. (2014). Global localities: Olympic bidding as a case study in globalization. *Sport in Society.* Taylor & Francis. doi:10.1080/17430437.2013.834626

Van der Wagen, L. (2007). *Human resource management for events: Managing the event workforce.* London: Routledge.

Weiler, J. (2011). *The evolution of 2010 legacies now a continuing legacy of the 2010 winter games through venture philanthropy.* Vancouver: Lift Partners.

Weiler, J., & Mohan, A. (2009). *Catalyst, collaborator, connector: The social innovation model of 2010 legacies now-case study.* Vancouver: Lift Partners.

Yukl, G. (1971). Toward a behavioral theory of leadership. *Organizational Behavior and Human Performance, 6*(4), 414–440.

6 Leadership practices from a diversity and inclusion perspective

Introduction

The terms diversity and inclusion have become part of the everyday vernacular in both the business and sport management environment. However, the realities of positive hiring practices and engaging leaders from diverse backgrounds in real ways that support and foster diversity and inclusive practices have tended to be lacking. This is affirmed by the perpetuation of leaders from similar backgrounds who do not alter the status quo but reinforce hegemonic practices of leadership. Embedded in the notions of leadership that support diversity and inclusion is the idea of social justice. This perspective is about disrupting social practices and breaking down hegemonic power structures to ensure that individuals from all backgrounds have access to leadership in sport organisations and that leadership processes foster an inclusive organisational environment.

In this chapter, we focus on leadership practices that support diversity and inclusion in sport organisations. The sport literature on specific practices that foster greater diversity in sport organisations is lacking; nonetheless there has been extensive research on the need to improve diversity throughout sport. This stems from a desire to foster a sporting environment that is more socially just and reflective of changing practices in society. We offer a number of theoretical approaches that might support more socially just organisations and consider the role of leaders in fostering diversity in sport. We argue that at the heart of socially just leadership is the principle of good character. We lay the foundation for thinking about leading for diversity on the strength of a leader's character. We argue that the concepts of emancipatory leadership, servant leadership, and leader character offer some understandings regarding unique approaches in considering the role of leaders in more diverse and inclusive organisations and sport environments that encourage and support more socially just practices.

Defining diversity and inclusion

A starting point that needs to be made clear in this work is how we define diversity in terms of understanding the concepts of leadership. We draw upon the conceptualisation of social diversity in organisations, which suggests that the social constructs of race, ethnicity, religious beliefs, socio-economic status, ability, language, geographical origin, gender, and/or sexual orientation are all valued and represented in a meaningful way. This perspective acknowledges that such social diversity is critical for delivering different knowledges, backgrounds, experiences, and interests that will benefit the organisation. This approach is important for considering that people have different customs related to time management, eating habits, organisational dress, etc. that require open-mindedness and a leader who is able to build a strong organisational culture that values difference. This dovetails with the concept of inclusion in terms of a leadership approach.

Inclusive organisations typically consist of diverse individuals and are often learning-centred organisations, which emphasise creativity and innovativeness valuing the distinct perspectives and contributions of all people (Cunningham, 2011). This often means implementing principles of universal design that accommodate all forms of diversity in the physical and organisational environment (Markel & Elia, 2016). Inclusive organisations recruit and retain diverse staff and volunteers to reflect the composition of the communities they serve, and this requires leaders with particular character traits and values that support this approach (as discussed in Chapter 2). It is here that there seems to be a paucity of research related to such diversity in the sport literature and even in the broader leadership literature. Hence, in the following section we highlight some of the sport-related work that has been completed on diversity/inclusion and leadership to highlight the gaps and offer some understandings of the learnings about such a perspective of leadership.

Background literature on diversity and leadership

Researchers have demonstrated that more diverse organisations foster more creativity and offer unique opportunities for the development of talent (Shore et al., 2011), and this perspective is at the heart of research around leadership diversity (e.g. Nielsen & Nielsen, 2013). Thus, we begin by considering the literature relating to leadership and diversity, and leadership and inclusion. Scholars in the past have generally used different definitions of diversity to frame their approaches and often focus on only one aspect of diversity. The business literature has advanced well beyond the narrow meanings of diversity to consider all different aspects of diverse leadership and organisations such as firm nationality, political climate, and sectoral diversity.

In the sport literature, much of the research has centred upon traditional understandings of diversity that point out the problematic perspectives of hegemonic practices in sport. One of the concerns with research on leadership and diverse practices is that all too often the measures used and the frameworks examined rely on previous research that has centred on white, male, heteronormative understandings of leadership. Thus, even the research itself can be highly problematic in perpetuating some of the normative practices around diversity and inclusion if there is not a shift to more inclusive practices as a whole. There are varying degrees of inclusionary and/or discriminatory practices in both the way sport organisations implement these practices and the ways in which researchers address evaluation. Further, we also want to note that while there is an immense amount of scholarly literature on diversity and leadership in sport, the concept of inclusion and leadership has received far less attention. Hence, we bring together these areas to highlight some of the future challenges around leadership practices that support diversity and inclusion. We aim to clarify the perspective that addresses diversity as not only the representation of leaders but also the practices of leadership that aim to foster more diverse and inclusive organisational environments. This approach is then about considering approaches that foster creativity and ingenuity in organisations. We suggest here that fostering a work culture that emphasises the importance of diversity and inclusion is a business imperative, and not just a moral or ethical one. A more diverse workforce will put any company into a stronger position to grow and innovate (Bunderson & Van Der Vegt, 2018). It will also help attract top industry talent and businesses to connect with their customers.

By far the most prevalent area of scholarship on leadership and diversity is about the gender gaps that still exist in most businesses. Many organisations lack regular and robust equity policies and programmes that support women through a talent pipeline. Mid-career female-identified individuals tend to leave organisations at a higher rate than men, and men tend to be hired at a much higher rate than women for mid-level organisational positions which can lead to leadership roles (Dixon & Breuning, 2005). Programmes that support extended leave time and flexibility in the workplace environment can help the retention of women, but these programmes are often challenging to implement effectively. Advancement systems and support mechanisms that attempt to build leaders are often based on models that can detract from diversity because of unconscious biases about reward structures and traditional perspectives regarding promotions that might be triggered by such things as family or parental leave. Research has demonstrated that women often feel liked but not necessarily respected in the work environment. They believe that they receive less social support to assume leadership roles. Ely, Ibarra, and Kolb (2011) noted for instance that:

> People see men as better fit for leadership roles partly because the paths to such roles were designed with men in mind; the belief that men are a better fit propels more men into leadership roles, which reinforces the perceptions that men are a better fit, leaving gendered practices intact. Thus, a challenge for women is to construct leader identities, despite the subtle barriers organisations erect to their leadership advancement.
>
> (p. 478)

Despite the potential for positive results in business, we still know little about how organisations can become more diverse and inclusive. Much of the sport studies literature on diversity and leadership has focussed on issues of representation rather than leadership that supports a diversity perspective. Thus, we begin

Table 6.1 Sport studies examining diversity, inclusion, and leadership

References	Focus	Context	Leadership findings
Ahn and Cunningham (2017)	Gender and leadership positions	National Olympic Committee	Women continue to be under-represented in key leadership positions in international sport, also leading to the poor promotion of girls' and women's sport. Women continue to be excluded from board roles, so their influence on decision-making, governing processes, and board outcomes becomes unclear.
Bimper (2017)	Race and leadership	Intercollegiate athletics	Athletic programmes should consider appointing a senior-level chief diversity officer (CDO) within the athletic department, who has an expertise in sociocultural issues (e.g. race) and sport.
Borland and Bruening (2010)	Race and coaching	Intercollegiate athletics, Division I	The culture of Division I athletics strongly encourages conformity with white male values. Members of marginalised groups must adopt these values if they hope to gain a leadership position. Designated recruiting has in some cases made the women feel like tokens. Division I assistant coaches specified access discrimination, lack of support, and prevalent stereotypes as barriers to leadership positions.
Bradbury (2013)	Race and leadership	European football clubs	Recommendation of positive action approaches, incorporating methods such as target setting, co-option, and quotas to address the disconnect between equality of opportunities and (in)equality of outcomes that are experienced by minority populations in all areas of social, economic, and political life. Emphasise developing and delivering an industry standard programme of cultural awareness and anti-discrimination training for senior administrators, directors, and executive committee members at professional clubs.
Burton, Welty Peachey, and Wells (2017)	Servant leadership	Intercollegiate athletics	Servant leadership should be highlighted and supported to facilitate ethical climates in sport organisations. Leaders of sport organisations should also focus on ways to enhance procedural justice within their organisation to help enhance organisational ethics, commitment, and diversity.

(Continued)

References	Focus	Context	Leadership findings
Cunningham (2009)	Coaching	NCAA Division I	Focusses on what steps coaches and administrators could take to decrease the potential negative effects of diversity (e.g. low life satisfaction). Emphasis on single entity membership is important for supporting diversity and work satisfaction. Diversity training should emphasise positive effects of diversity.
Cunningham and Sagas (2004)	Coaching	NCAA Division I	Administrators must support department environments that not only accept diversity, but they must also see the value in such workforce heterogeneity in order to assemble and retain a diverse coaching staff. This research suggests that cultures of diversity are needed to recruit, attract, and retain a diverse ensemble of coaches.
Day (2015)	Race and coaching	Intercollegiate athletics	Job-level, task-based segregation may be one key process that keeps minorities' abilities from being recognised equal to those of whites and, therefore, perpetuates racial and ethnic inequality in career mobility. Recommendations focus on diversity programmes to include networking opportunities for minority coaches with current leaders within the profession.
Lieberman and Shaw (2012)	Gender and leadership	National sport organisations	Relationship building, stakeholder management, self-awareness, and sense of judgement were critical to success in the sports industry for female sport leaders. Confirmed the importance mentors can have in terms of combatting the established "Old Boy's" networks that often exist in the sport industry.
Palmer and Masters (2010)	Māori women sport leaders	National sport organisations	Participants reflected a hybrid style of leadership that embraced their ethnocultural perspective. Support through mentors and support networks was important in a male-dominated, highly competitive setting. They all experienced institutional racism, sexism, and marginalisation due to their ethnocultural and gendered identities as well as limited resources and lack of support from governing bodies.

Reference	Topic	Context	Summary
Schull, Shaw, and Kihl (2013)	Gender and leadership positions	Intercollegiate athletics	Gender equity criteria, while seemingly gender-neutral, privilege a certain type of masculinity in the sport context: a man who values gender equity. Results also revealed that search practices and politics, like all organisational processes, are gendered. Organisations must be aware of how specific gendered processes operate within the organisation to create inequities.
Shaw and Hoeber (2003)	Gender and leadership positions	National sport organisations	The findings suggest that senior management roles are heavily dominated by discourses of masculinity linked to men and are highly valued in sport organisations. In contrast, women and discourses of femininity are associated with employment roles that are undervalued within sport organisations. There is a need to develop equity with respect to the discourses that inform employment roles in sport organisations.
van Knippenberg, van Ginkel, and Homan (2013)	Diversity mindsets and team diversity	Sport organisations	Current diversity training most commonly practised will fail to improve the accuracy, sharedness, and awareness of sharedness of diversity mindsets. The authors call on organisations to shift the focus of practice to people's appreciation of diversity as something that should be understood to actually creating diversity in their work teams. A change needs to occur in HR practices for leadership development specifically focussing more attention on developing leaders' understanding of and efforts towards the development of accurate diversity mindsets.
Walker and Bopp (2010)	Gender and coaching	NCAA Division I	The perceived opportunity of women to sustain and pursue careers in male-dominated workplaces (e.g. men's college basketball) was negatively influenced by the perception of gendered opportunities, male-exclusive social networks, and from pressures to overcompensate for being female. Women therefore believe that societal, structural, and organisational changes need to be determined in order for women to actively pursue and successfully obtain positions in male-dominated workplaces.

by discussing what has been examined in the literature to consider the gaps and possibilities for expanding into present understanding of new domains around issues of diversity and leadership. We then draw upon theoretical approaches to considering the character of leaders to show how this perspective offers interesting considerations regarding the role of leaders in creating more diverse and inclusive organisations. Fundamentally, we argue that at the heart of inclusion and diversity is good character traits that foster such an approach.

Diversity and sport leadership

As outlined throughout this book, research in sport and leadership has been approached from a number of different diversity perspectives and in varied organisational contexts. However, there is a rather limited stream of literature that focusses on leadership specifically, as much of the literature examines broader issues of organisational culture, managerial role clarity, and athlete influences – all of which do have an impact on leadership. Table 6.1 presents a summary of some of the sport studies that focus specifically on diversity and leadership. Notably absent from the review is the concept of leadership and practices of inclusion in the sporting space.

The most common area of sport research has been on gender and leadership. This spans leadership roles as related to coaching on the one hand to CEOs of major sport corporations on the other hand. A common thread that runs through this research is that sport organisations have often been places that reproduce traditional gender roles and privilege masculinity. Much of the literature on gender and leadership in sport has shown that despite advances in some workplaces, on the whole, women are under-represented in leadership positions, receive less compensation for their work than their male counterparts, and are often marginalised in the workplace (Cunningham, 2008; Cunningham & Sagas, 2008; Kihl, Leberman & Schull, 2010).

Sport is often laden with gendered norms reproducing the masculine ideals (Schull, Shaw, & Kihl, 2013) as key to leadership and thus remains a challenging place for those identifying as women in terms of leadership roles. The status quo in sport organisations has long dominated the landscape of sport leadership, which is typically white, heterosexual, and male. The maintenance of this status quo has perpetuated in terms of attitudes, values, and leadership priorities for those in leadership positions in sport (Fink & Pastore, 1999). What much of the literature on the under-representation of women in leadership positions in sport suggests is that the gender-role meanings and stereotypes associated with social and sport ideology have also functioned to limit the capacity of females within the sport context.

In a special issue of the journal *Sex Roles*, sport management scholars focussed on the issues of gender and sport, demonstrating a continued perpetuation of the heterosexual masculine understanding of sport as the ideal type. Hoeber (2008), for instance, highlighted the entrenchment of inequities and negative attitudes among athletes and coaches that serve to marginalise others and perpetuate the peripheral role of female leaders. Without women in leadership roles supporting changes in workplace culture, the sporting environment also negatively impacts female coaches (Dixon & Breuning, 2007). Further negative perceptions of female athletes from their male counterparts and general public demonstrate the challenging cultural environment in which gender roles exist and perpetuate entrenched power imbalances. This leads to a vicious cycle where gender roles are reproduced in the sporting environment and demonstrated through those in leadership positions.

Sartore and Cunningham (2007) have argued that the traditional models upon which sport organisations function fail to empower women to view themselves as adequate and appropriate leaders and/or coaches, thus further propagating the under-representation and lack of diversity. Drawing upon identity theory and identity control processes, they argue that this behaviour can all too often be self-limiting and further reproduce the masculine ideal-type leadership in organisations. The impact of this over time is that it results in organisations continually lacking in diversity. In Canada, there certainly have been advances in the representation of women in leadership positions, but there is still room for a great deal of improvement. As reported by Kidd in 2013:

> Only six of the 19-person executive (31.5%) of the Canadian Olympic Committee (COC) are female; only five of the 15-person board (33%) of the Coaching Association of Canada (CAC) are female; only four members of the 13-member board (30.7%) for the 2015 Pan/Parapan American Games are female. Only 17% of the Athletic Director positions in Canadian universities are held by women.
>
> (p. 2)

In professional sport, the level of diversity is even lower. In Canadian professional sport, there are 58 Vice-President (VP) positions or higher. Only seven women occupy these positions, which represents only 12% of people in VP roles. These numbers demonstrate some movement from the previous decades but certainly validate the continued under-representation of women in senior sport leadership positions. This trend continues, despite policy efforts on behalf of the Canadian federal government to support female leadership development and women and girls' participation in sport more broadly. The Canadian policy *Actively Engaged: A Policy on Sport for Women and Girls* (2009) highlighted the persistent concerns that women's contributions to Canadian sport continue to be undervalued by women themselves as well as by their male counterparts. Further, "the availability of women to contribute to the sport system tends to be constrained because of societal expectations on women to fulfill traditional domestic roles – including responsibility for domestic tasks to facilitate the contribution to sport by their male partners" (p. 1).

The policy is aimed at promoting innovative strategies to build and develop female leaders in the sport system through targeted recruitment, development strategies, and retention programmes which also recognise the importance of re-recruiting women into similar or other sport roles after a hiatus (e.g. parental leaves). Furthermore, there is movement in attempting to understand the intersectionality of marginality in leadership, where transgendered individuals, women of diverse racial backgrounds, and women experiencing disability are all under-represented in leadership. Innovative ideas and approaches need to be developed to ensure more equitable opportunities to improve the sport experiences for all people.

Palmer and Masters (2010) research on Māori women sport leaders is particularly interesting in terms of the barriers and challenges faced by women in leadership positions in sport. Their experiences highlight the male-dominated, highly competitive sport environment where institutional racism, sexism, and marginalisation is prevalent. They faced further challenges due to their ethnocultural and gendered identities, which is often exacerbated by the limited resources and support from the sport governing bodies. Nonetheless, these women also demonstrated the opportunities to navigate the system by gaining access into social networks, mentors, and challenging the ethnocultural stereotypes. These leaders also brought new insights to the fore by advancing a quadruple bottom line agenda which valued the economic, environmental, social, and cultural aspects of success. This type of new perspective is demonstrative of the importance of diverse leadership and workplace practices. It should be noted, however, that Palmer and Masters's (2010) work also demonstrated that the added challenges of navigating an institutional racist environment and bringing new cultural insights to understanding organisational success come at a significant cost in terms of leadership burnout.

Research that examines the diversity of leadership in sport organisations is severely lacking and thus little is known about the racial and ethnic diversity of sport leaders. The limited evidence points to a similar trend, as seen in gender perspectives, where leaders tend to be heterosexual white male, fitting with the sporting cultural ideal. Bradbury's (2013) work on football in Europe is telling about the institutionalised racism in leadership positions. His analysis of key stakeholders' perceptions across 20 countries demonstrated a culture of overt racism and institutional norms that perpetuate discriminatory practices in the sport and which limited the potential for broadening the leadership landscape. This research echoes the work of others such as Burdsey (2004), who demonstrated additional patterns of racism in football that are also prevalent across multiple levels of senior leadership positions in the sport.

In terms of other forms of diversity in leadership research, there remains a significant gap in understanding the nature, roles, responsibilities, and opportunities for change. The perpetuation of unequal patterns of social relations is exacerbated by the homogeneity of the sporting environment, which is regulated by the socio-historical trajectories of sport. The nature and culture of the sporting environment tend to preclude anyone from leading organisations that does not fit the ideal typical model. In many countries, newcomers, the cultural and religious distinctiveness of some minority groups, and the limited educational and language skills of many first-generation migrants can present significant challenges to addressing the context of diversity in sport. Even in countries that feature a range of more established and relatively integrated second- and third-generation minority populations (e.g. Canada, the United Kingdom), there seems to be continued structural discrimination, sustained social and economic disadvantage, and shared experiences of social exclusion in sport that are evidenced by the lack of diversity in leadership positions.

In order to challenge the ongoing exclusionary practices in sport leadership, there needs to be a much greater concerted effort at challenging institutional racism and gender biases to promote more equitable and inclusionary practices to open up leadership opportunities in sport. Sport organisations need to recognise diversity as a positive resource that benefits their organisations. Research from the business literature has demonstrated that companies with more women in senior management positions and on boards of directors, as well as those with more ethnic minorities in leadership roles, perform better overall (Curtis, Schmid, & Struber, 2012; Krishnan & Park, 2005; Nielsen & Nielsen, 2013). Herring (2009) demonstrated that commercially oriented for-profit businesses that value diversity increase revenues, increase their customer base, and achieve greater relative profits. Furthermore, Nielsen and Nielsen (2013) have found that nationality diversity is directly associated with firm performance. Thus, the question remains how to promote more diversity in leadership when sport organisations are so completely embedded in a white male heteronormative sporting culture.

Coaching and diversity

Coaching is an important aspect of leadership in the sport environment. In terms of coaching, there also remains a significant gap in relation to diversity of representation in many sports and disciplines. Efforts have been made in many countries to invest in coaching programmes that support females and those from diverse backgrounds; however, the gender gap and racial divides still perpetuate. The challenge stems from a similar position where the culture of sport tends to reflect a white male heteronormative approach. Coaching models are embedded with these cultural assumptions. Hoeber (2008) demonstrated that the meanings around equity and equality in intercollegiate athletics were mixed and poorly implemented. She noted that the lack of recognition of diverse perspectives can stem from both men and women in the system who have been acculturated in the heteronormative male understandings of sport. This can be done intentionally as a way to protect one's own position within the systems but also as a lack of resources that reflect diverse coaching practices.

Cunningham (2009a) noted that in environments where diversity is being achieved to a greater degree in coaching, there are challenges associated with this approach that need to be navigated. He has argued that emphasising the positive aspects of diverse coaching perspectives in training alongside support for diversity among senior leadership can help foster greater work satisfaction. This will help foster cultures of diversity and improve overall representation and culture change to promote diversity and inclusion (Cunningham & Sagas, 2008). An interesting perspective on the coaching piece is the issue of role clarity and attainment, despite the improved representation of minority groups into coaching. Day (2015) investigated job tasks, segregation, and organisational mobility for United States college football coaches. He determined that black coaches are disproportionately placed in non-central positions that inhibit upward mobility and receive discrepancy in return for being in central or upwardly mobile positions relative to white coaches. This highlights issues of job-level segregation that inhibit leadership opportunities and continued racialisation of coaching in sport. This creates challenges for supporting more diverse and inclusive sporting environments.

Advancing diversity and inclusion through leadership

Human resource models around diversity are often most strongly aligned multiculturalist and integrationist approaches that seek to manage diversity and promote intercultural exchange through levelling of barriers of association (van Knippenberg, van Ginkel, & Homan, 2013). However, there is limited research that actually addresses defined steps in terms of advancing the thinking of leading to support more diverse and inclusive organisations. Certainly, some of the research in sport studies has emphasised the importance of mentors and supportive partnerships in navigating the male heteronormative culture of sport. Other studies have also addressed the need for diversity training in organisations and policies that support an inclusive climate, but these remain a challenge to developing diverse sport leadership. Ultimately, changing the power structures in sporting environments that support diverse and inclusive leadership practices need to centre on a social justice approach. This approach is about legitimacy, fairness, and equitable distribution of goods and responsibilities (Burton, Welty Peachey, & Wells, 2017). This approach is built on a foundation where people are meaningfully included in institutional practices and processes. It is through such an approach that leaders can enable more socially inclusive practices and ensure more people are included in organisational decision-making.

But, typically, leadership and social justice do not coincide in many of the traditional approaches to understanding leader practices and behaviours. This is because traditional leadership approaches reinforce normative understandings of culture, inclusion, and opportunity, particularly in sport. Hierarchical practices of leadership in business and sport often preclude socially inclusive practices that support a social justice lens. Power remains within singular positions or with individuals, which has the impact of precluding more inclusive practices due to the exclusion of other voices, values, and perspectives. The ethos of efficiency and productivity do little to promote inclusion unless leadership practices specifically target these areas.

Theories of leadership that support more inclusive practice tend to reject hierarchical or overly bureaucratic views of managing organisations and leadership approaches. Because these hierarchical approaches tend to reflect or reinforce unjust societal hierarchies of gender, class, race, and ethnicity, more socially just approaches must be articulated. For leadership to be genuinely inclusive, it must foster equitable and horizontal relationships that also transcend wider gender, race, and class divisions. This often reflects leadership approaches that favour more collective characteristics. In the following section, we review a number of alternative perspectives for considering inclusive and socially just practices of leadership that promote more diverse sporting environments.

Emancipatory leadership

Corson (2000) introduced the concept of emancipatory leadership in educational settings as a means to consider the complex sociocultural environment in which education takes place. This approach recognises that those within the environment might have greater knowledge and expertise about the complexity of situations and ought to have a greater role in decision-making processes. Furthermore, decision-making does not rely solely on an individual leader but extends that decision authority to those who have a stake in the outcome. The leader also takes a back seat to the process, removing themselves from the power effects that bind their leadership, ensuring the voice of those being served come to the forefront. From a similar perspective, Ashraf (2010) has argued that diversity of thought and sense-making around the ideals set forth by those most impacted by decisions shift the leader-centred paradigm and enable societal values such as civic engagement, social cohesion, and responsive governance.

In a comparable vein, feminist practices of leadership with a 'women-centred' approach have also been considered under this emancipatory perspective. From this standpoint women can be active and creative in constructing their own leadership practices to effectively meet the needs of their constituents. The underlying notion of emancipatory leadership is that leadership resides in the communities being served rather than in one single person. Thus, leadership is not a function of a position but represents a conjunction where behaviours, decisions, and ideas are shared between leaders and followers (Brown, 2004). This is an important approach in changing the culture of an environment with longstanding, ingrained hegemonic values such as sport. This tactic is likely very important for an inclusive approach within educational settings and non-profit sectors of sport but might not be an adequate approach for the business sector where governance emphasises profitability and winning. This approach requires time and an immense amount of collective effort to change the power structures and move inclusive practices throughout the organisation. It offers an alternative and valuable perspective on considering inclusive leadership practices.

Servant leadership

Some in the sport management space have discussed the idea that servant leadership might be an approach to considering the redistribution of power and provide opportunities for more inclusive practices (see the following chapter for a detailed examination of servant leadership in the context of sport for development). Servant leadership as a theory emerged from Robert Greenleaf's (1977) work, which argued that the servant leader's primary mission is to serve: "It begins with the natural feeling that one wants to serve, to serve first. Then, conscious choice brings one to aspire to lead" (p. 10). The premise was built upon the challenges of previous leadership theories which suggest that leaders that aspire to lead first, rather than serve, in order to gain or retain power. In this case, the emphasis on the individual leader's characteristics is at the heart of the desires for power or to serve others in a more inclusive manner. Patterson (2003) furthered this theory by emphasising the virtues upon which serving others is based. The central characteristics upon which leadership from a servant perspective are based are: (1) leads and serves with love, (2) acts with humility, (3) is altruistic, (4) is visionary for the followers, (5) is trusting, (6) is serving, and (7) empowers followers (Winston & Patterson, 2006).

While there are some similarities to the concept of transformational leadership, some have argued that the personal growth of followers is primarily viewed within the context of organisational success (Graham, 1991). This leaves open the possibility of manipulating followers and employees in order to meet organisational goals or the leader's personal goals. The concept of servant leadership is believed to be more grounded in an ethical framework that emphasises the importance of social justice. Burton, Welty Peachey, and Wells (2017) found that a servant leadership style by athletic directors in intercollegiate athletic departments led to perceptions of a more socially just and ethical environment. These findings align with research in related fields suggesting that the unique attributes of servant leaders can help foster a more ethical working climate. Further, this style of leadership recognises the unique attributes of servant leadership as a style of leadership that can foster an ethical sporting environment with a culture of inclusive practices. This in turn is more likely to foster diverse environments where different perspectives are valued and believed to be essential in developing wider organisational goals. The embedded processes of procedural justice can present the opportunity for sport to develop in a more ethical climate that fosters innovation, celebrates difference, and empowers marginalised others.

Leader character

In direct relation to the previous two theoretical perspectives is the concept of leader character. It is here that we argue there is an opportunity to make the most impact on diversity and inclusion in the workplace and ultimately in leadership. Crossan et al. (2017) have worked towards developing a framework of leader character that could help support organisations including those in sport understand the necessary character traits of a leader to drive forward an ethical and virtuous agenda. This idea sits well in sport organisations where there has been much controversy over ethical concerns such as doping, bribery, and money laundering. Additionally, the concept of leader character that offers insights into considering diversity in an organisation is the expansion to concepts beyond traditional normative considerations of leadership. Crossan et al. (2017) draw upon the notion that leader character is a contextually specific moral component that is related but separate from values and personality, and can be developed in people. An important consideration herein is that character as discussed by Crossan et al. is contextual and culturally dictated. Thus, while often social identity theorists (as described in Chapter 2) critique character in relation to the group context, character from a social justice perspective aims to emphasise social and contextual understandings of character.

This work aligns with the notion of virtuous character, where the habits of cognition, emotion, and behaviour embody human excellence and are able to produce a more socially just organisation and society. Virtues ultimately work as values which situate the direction of a leader and an organisation. A leader must value diversity and opportunity for all for the ethos of inclusion to become embedded in the way that organisations function. This impacts the manner in how they work towards achieving their central mission while also fostering a more virtuous working environment. Senior sport leaders should lead by example and affirm, through what they say and what they reward regarding diverse and inclusive practices, those who exhibit the requisite behaviours and explain how these practices contribute to personal and organisational success (Crossan et al., 2017). Through this approach, sport organisations might begin to foster more diverse working environments.

Conclusion

There is likely no simple answer to creating a more diverse and inclusive organisational environment in sport. Leaders themselves play a key role in supporting and valuing diversity in sport organisations. They need to be clear about their own expectations and ensure that sport can offer a more integrated and sustainable setting. However, leadership is wrought with the challenges of perpetuating the wrongs of the past because of the ingrained understandings, meaning, and values laden in the broader sport environment. Consider that organisations such as the International Paralympic Committee have no policy on organisational leadership regarding experiences and understandings of disability. In Canada, the CEO of the Canadian Paralympic Committee is a strong woman who defies the gender constraints prevalent in the Canadian sport system, but representation of individuals with disabilities is almost entirely absent from an organisation that serves athletes with disabilities. As alluded to in this chapter and throughout the book, the problems continue to be pervasive across the whole of sport. While there need to be policies, education, and procedures in place for ensuring more equitable and diverse sport, where these do exist, there still remain ongoing challenges for inclusion and diversity. Leaders will need to be bold, take steps to ensure diversity, and potentially give up their own agency and power to make way for honouring and ensuring diversity. This social justice lens is what will help make sport a diverse place, and leaders are the key to making this happen.

We have offered a number of models to consider in terms of leadership and diversity, but it will take a great deal more research and understanding of the cultural environment to foster leadership that truly supports diversity and ultimately changes the faces of leadership in sport. Policies need to ensure fair opportunity for employment and leadership planning. These need to encourage a diverse perspective of qualifications for leadership. Most models of leadership remain embedded in a white male model with little understanding of other approaches that would support sporting efforts for more diverse leadership. Reward systems, hiring practices, and ultimately the culture of sport will need to shift if we expect to have more leaders in sport that represent a broad spectrum of diversity.

References

Ahn, N. Y., & Cunningham, G. B. (2017). Cultural values and gender equity on National Olympic Committee boards. *International Journal of Exercise Science, 10*(6), 857–874.

Ashraf, N. (2010). Emancipatory leadership: A framework for understanding exclusion in organizational decision-making. *Canadian Journal of Social Research, 3*(2), 58–67.

Bimper, Jr., A. Y. (2017). Mentorship of black student-athletes at a predominately white American university: Critical race theory perspective on student-athlete development. *Sport, Education and Society, 22*(2), 175–193.

Borland, J. F., & Bruening, J. E. (2010). Navigating barriers: A qualitative examination of the under-representation of black females as head coaches in collegiate basketball. *Sport Management Review, 13*(4), 407–420.

Bradbury, S. (2013). Institutional racism, whiteness and the under-representation of minorities in leadership positions in football in Europe. *Soccer & Society, 14*(3), 296–314.

Brown, K. (2004). Leadership for social justice and equity: Weaving a transformative framework and pedagogy. *Educational Administration Quarterly, 40*(1), 77–108.

Bunderson, J. S., & Van Der Vegt, G. S. (2018). Annual review of organizational psychology and organizational behavior diversity and inequality in management teams: A review and integration of research on vertical and horizontal member differences. *Annual Review of Organizational Psychology and Organizational Behavior, 5*, 47–73.

Burdsey, D. (2004). Obstacle race? 'Race', racism and the recruitment of British Asian professional footballers. *Patterns of Prejudice, 38*(3), 279–299.

Burton, L. J., Welty Peachey, J., & Wells, J. E. (2017). The role of servant leadership in developing an ethical climate in sport organizations. *Journal of Sport Management, 31*(3), 229–240.

Corson, D. (2000). *Language diversity and education.* London: Routledge.

Crossan, M. M., Byrne, A., Seijts, G. H., Reno, M., Monzani, L., & Gandz, J. (2017). Toward a framework of leader character in organizations. *Journal of Management Studies, 54*(7), 986–1018. doi:10.1111/joms.12254

Cunningham, G. B. (2008). Creating and sustaining gender diversity in sport organizations. *Sex Roles.* doi:10.1007/s11199-007-9312-3

Cunningham, G. B. (2009a). Examining the relationship among coaching staff diversity, perceptions of diversity, value congruence, and life satisfaction. *Research Quarterly for Exercise and Sport, 80*, 326–335.

Cunningham, G. B. (2009b). Understanding the diversity-related change process: A field study. *Journal of Sport Management, 23,* 407–428.

Cunningham, G. B. (2011). Creative work environments in sport organizations: The influence of sexual orientation diversity and commitment to diversity. *Journal of Homosexuality, 58*(8), 1041–1057.

Cunningham, G. B., & Sagas, M. (2004). People make the difference: The influence of the coaching staff's human capital and diversity on team performance. *European Sport Management Quarterly, 4*(1), 3–21.

Cunningham, G. B., & Sagas, M. (2008). Gender and sex diversity in sport organizations: Introduction to a special issue. *Sex Roles, 58*(1–2), 3–9.Curtis, M., Schmid, C., & Struber, M. (2012). *Gender diversity and corporate performance.* Credit Suisse: Research Institute.

Day, J. C. (2015). Transitions to the top: Race, segregation, and promotions to executive positions in the college football coaching profession. *Work and Occupations, 42*(4), 408–446.

Dixon, M. A., & Bruening, J. E. (2005). Perspectives on work-family conflict in sport: An integrated approach. *Sport Management Review, 8*(3), 227–253.

Dixon, M. A., & Bruening, J. E. (2007). Work–family conflict in coaching I: A top-down perspective. *Journal of Sport Management, 21*(3), 377–406.

Ely, R. J., Ibarra, H., & Kolb, D. M. (2011). Taking gender into account: Theory and design for women's leadership development programs. *Academy of Management Learning & Education, 10*(3), 474–493.

Fink, J. S., & Pastore, D. L. (1999). Diversity in sport? Utilizing the business literature to devise a comprehensive framework of diversity initiatives. *Quest.* doi:10.1080/0033 6297.1999.10491688

Graham, J. W. (1991). Servant-leadership in organizations: Inspirational and moral. *The Leadership Quarterly, 2*(2), 105–119.

Greenleaf, R. K. (1997). *The servant as leader.* Notre Dame, IN: University of Notre Dame Press.

Herring, C. (2009). Does diversity pay?: Race, gender, and the business case for diversity. *American Sociological Review, 74*(2), 208–224. doi:10.1177/000312240907400203

Hoeber, L. (2008). Gender equity for athletes: Multiple understandings of an organizational value. *Sex Roles, 58*(1–2), 58–71.

Kihl, L. A., Leberman, S., & Schull, V. (2010). Stakeholder constructions of leadership in intercollegiate athletics. *European Sport Management Quarterly, 10,* 241–270.

Krishnan, H. A., & Park, D. (2005). A few good women—on top management teams. *Journal of Business Research, 58*(12), 1712–1720.

Leberman, S., & Shaw, S. (2012). Preparing female sport management students for leadership roles in sport. Report for Ako Aotearoa, Wellington.

Markel, K. S., & Elia, B. (2016). How human resource management can best support employees with autism: Future directions for research and practice. *Journal of Business and Management, 22*(1), 71–85.

Nielsen, B. B., & Nielsen, S. (2013). Top management team nationality diversity and firm performance: A multilevel study. *Strategic Management Journal, 34*(3), 373–382. doi:10.1002/smj.2021

Palmer, F. R., & Masters, T. M. (2010). Māori feminism and sport leadership: Exploring Māori women's experiences. *Sport Management Review, 13*(4), 331–344. doi:10.1016/J.SMR.2010.06.001

Patterson, K. (2003). Servant leadership: A theoretical model. *Dissertation Abstracts International, 64*(02), 570.

Sartore, M. L., & Cunningham, G. B. (2007). Explaining the under-representation of women in leadership positions of sport organizations: A symbolic interactionist perspective. *Quest, 59*(2), 244–265.

Schull, V., Shaw, S., & Kihl, L. A. (2013). "If a woman came in... she would have been eaten alive": Analyzing gendered political processes in the search for an athletic director. *Gender & Society, 27*, 56–81.

Shaw, S., & Hoeber, L. (2003). "A strong man is direct and a direct woman is a bitch": Gendered discourses and their influence on employment roles in sport organizations. *Journal of Sport Management, 17*(4), 347–375.

Shore, L. M., Randel, A. E., Chung, B. G., Dean, M. A., Ehrhart, K. H., & Singh, G. (2011). Inclusion and diversity in work groups: A review and model for future research. *Journal of Management, 37*, 1262–1289.

van Knippenberg, D., van Ginkel, W. P., & Homan, A. C. (2013). Diversity mindsets and the performance of diverse teams. *Organizational Behavior and Human Decision Processes, 121*(2), 183–193.

Walker, N. A., & Bopp. T. (2010). The under-representation of women in the male-dominated workplace: Perspectives of female coaches. *Journal of Workplace Rights, 15*, 47–64.

Winston, B. E., & Patterson, K. (2006). An integrative definition of leadership. *International Journal of Leadership Studies, 1*(2), 6–66.

7 Leadership and sport-for-development (SFD)

Introduction

The field of sport-for-development (SFD) has been presented as an innovative, active, and engaging approach to community development. In short, SFD is defined as the intentional "use of sport to exert a positive influence on public health, the socialisation of children, youths and adults, the social inclusion of the disadvantaged, the economic development of regions and states, and on fostering intercultural exchange and conflict resolution" (Lyras & Welty Peachey, 2011, p. 311). In contrast to traditional forms of sport development that focus on improving athletes' skills and talent, SFD programmes are designed to benefit people from disadvantaged backgrounds through sport-based community development activities. As such, SFD goes beyond the delivery of sport itself and aims to contribute to improvements in people's well-being by advancing social, cultural, economic, educational, and health-related aspects of community life (Levermore & Beacom, 2009; Schulenkorf & Adair, 2014; Sherry, Schulenkorf, & Phillips, 2016).

Over the past 15 years, SFD has received increased attention from both practitioners and academics around the world. Back in 2001, the creation of the United Nations Office for Sport for Development and Peace (UNOSDP) was the first significant step towards official recognition and legitimacy for SFD. Subsequent assertions, such as the Magglingen Declaration in 2003 and the United Nation's International Year of Sport and Physical Education in 2005, further raised awareness of SFD as a philosophy underpinning aspirations for positive change (Burnett, 2015; Schulenkorf & Adair, 2014). Since then, the increased awareness of potential social, health, and economic benefits resulting from SFD has led to the creation of thousands of local and international development projects supported and/or implemented by non-governmental organisations (NGOs), government departments, sport associations, aid agencies, and funding bodies around the world.

Overall, contemporary SFD research indicates that sport *can* play a significant role in local and international development; however, the use of sport for development purposes is neither simple nor inherently successful, and "success" often depends on the specific design, management, and leadership of SFD projects (Coalter, 2010, 2013; Darnell & Black, 2011; Schulenkorf, 2017). In this chapter, we focus specifically on the leadership aspects of SFD. We look at the most relevant leadership theory and recent scholarship in the SFD field, present a case study around sport and leadership challenges in a Pacific Islands context, and discuss future opportunities to advance research and practice in SFD leadership.

Leadership theories that underpin SFD programmes

While leadership is arguably one of the most researched topics in the field of business studies, the concept still needs to be fully deciphered and understood in a wider SFD context. In the chapter on Leadership Development, we learned that McCall (2010) described leadership as a truly complex and culturally influenced phenomenon. This also means that leadership in the context of SFD – where projects are often orchestrated by various local and international stakeholders – is an area of significant importance, particularly given that effective leadership is likely to present a competitive advantage for people, communities, and organisations (Day, 2000). In SFD, where projects often rely on individual 'cause champions', 'change agents', or dedicated community leaders to generate and maintain momentum (see Cohen & Welty Peachey, 2015; Edwards, 2015; Schulenkorf, 2010, 2012), a good understanding and application of leadership skills is critical for effective operations in the present and future. Against this background, this chapter focusses on two types of leadership theories that have been increasingly investigated and employed in the SFD space, namely 'servant leadership' and 'shared leadership'. Both of these leadership theories are designed to help organisations provide a social service; in doing so, they are not only looking inwards to support leadership staff but also looking outwards as they are geared towards helping and empowering relevant partners, stakeholders, and communities.

Servant leadership

Perhaps more than any other leadership theory, servant leadership explicitly emphasises the needs of engaging in leader-follower relationships (Patterson, 2003). While 'influence' is generally considered the central element of any leadership style, servant leadership changes the focus of this influence by emphasising the ideal of service in the leader-follower relationship. In view of current demands for more ethical, people-centred, and sustainable management in the sports industry, leadership inspired by the ideas from servant leadership theory may very well be what SFD organisations need. In other words, servant leadership has great potential and relevance in the SFD space, where projects are often underpinned by their social foci and drive towards local empowerment.

The term servant leadership was initially coined by Robert Greenleaf (1904–1990) in his seminal work "The Servant as Leader", first published in 1970. In his subsequent book, Greenleaf (1977) stated:

> The Servant-Leader is servant first … It begins with the natural feeling that one wants to serve, to serve first. Then conscious choice brings one to aspire

to lead … The best test, and difficult to administer is this: Do those served grow as persons? Do they, while being served, become healthier, wiser, freer, more autonomous, and more likely themselves to become servants? And, what is the effect on the least privileged in society? Will they benefit, or at least not further be harmed?

(p. 7)

This statement might be the most well-known quote in the servant leadership field. In short, Greenleaf proposed that service for people ought to be the distinguishing characteristic of leadership. Not only would it create a better, stronger society, but leaders would find greater joy in their lives if they raised the servant aspect of their practice and in doing so, create more serving institutions and just societies. Building on these ideals – and in an attempt to put more structure around Greenleaf's thoughts of what a service leader should look like – van Dierendonck (2011) engaged in a comprehensive review and synthesis on servant leadership skills. In particular, he identified and discussed six key characteristics that servant leaders (should) display. These are:

1   A servant leader **empowers their followers** and generates self-confidence and independence in the people they lead, encourages innovation, and acknowledges and fosters the abilities of their followers.
2   Servant leaders **practice humility,** in that they put their own accomplishments aside for the benefit of the organisation, acknowledge and seek out the contributions of others, and retreat into the background once their task is accomplished.
3   **Interpersonal acceptance**. Servant leaders understand the feelings and perspectives of others, they don't hold grudges but treat mistakes, arguments, and offences with compassion and forgiveness, and foster an environment of trust where mistakes are met with acceptance, not rejection.
4   **Providing direction**. Servant leaders clearly demonstrate what is expected of their followers and provide accountability and can customise directions based on follower's abilities, needs, and input.
5   **Authenticity** in public and personal life. A servant leader should do what is promised, be visible, and lead by example.
6   **Stewardship**. Servant leaders put the interests of the organisation over their own and above their own self-interests and set an example that can inspire others. This is closely linked with the concepts of teamwork, social responsibility, and loyalty.

Taken together, these six key characteristics are considered to have significant positive impacts on 'followers' to achieve self-actualisation, positive job attitudes, performance, and a stronger organisational focus on sustainability and corporate social responsibility. For these reasons, Welty Peachey and Burton (2017) argue that servant leadership is perhaps the most appropriate leadership style in SFD. Specifically, they suggest that "participants in sport development programs require a leader who is adept at nurturing, caring for, and empowering followers" (Welty Peachey & Burton, 2017, p. 126) and that these empowering attributes and strategies are essential for the long-term stability of SDP organisations. Welty Peachey and Burton (2017) go on to propose six aspects that the study of servant leadership can contribute to SFD management:

1   It will demonstrate compassionate love, gratitude, humility, altruism, and forgiveness to followers.
2   It will be effective in empowering followers.
3   It will foster a more sustainable organisation.
4   It will facilitate organisational effectiveness.
5   It will enhance the psychological satisfaction of followers/members.
6   Because of point 1, servant leaders will help diffuse power issues and control that could undermine the organisation.

A central argument presented by Welty Peachey and Burton (2017) is that servant leadership is less directed towards leading or engaging with the participants of an SFD programme but rather focusses on the *internal* organisational structure, aiming to support, train, inspire, and grow the abilities of staff members and volunteers from the inside out.

Shared leadership

Another relevant theory that has been discussed in an SFD context is 'shared leadership'; in short, it has been defined as

> a dynamic, interactive influence process among individuals in groups for which the objective is to lead one another to the achievement of group or organisational goals or both. This influence process often involves peer, or lateral, influence and at other times involves upward or downward hierarchical influence.
>
> (Pearce & Conger, 2003, p. 1)

In an SFD context, it has been argued that shared leadership will be effective for the following reasons:

1   It will improve an organisation's performance and effectiveness.
2   It encourages inclusive and balanced decision-making processes where knowledge is actively exchanged among all stakeholders.
3   It encourages creativity and the ability to implement innovative solutions over time.
4   It encourages an ethical climate among stakeholders, resulting in more ethical behaviour.

Overall, shared leadership is a useful model for SFD because programmes often require different people and organisations with distinct backgrounds and areas of expertise to come together. This includes the areas of sport, social work, conflict resolution, health, education, and so on. Across all these areas, shared leadership builds on the personal values, abilities, and personalities of individual leaders as important factors for organisational success. Thus, if the right group of leaders engage in reciprocal commitment and strong communication, the stage is set for a productive implementation of SFD projects. In other words, in the desire to achieve the best outcomes for SFD participants, shared leadership – if implemented collectively and inclusively – may well result in a competitive advantage for SFD programmes, given the combined strength of expert contributors (Kang & Svensson, 2018).

A critical aspect of shared leadership is the sociocultural environment. In 2018, Jones et al. (2018) conducted a multilevel analysis of shared leadership around a case study of the US-based SFD organisation Wakefield Youth Sports. Their findings suggested that environmental factors impact leadership development opportunities and that they are particularly "salient for SFP projects, considering they often operate in distressed and underserved communities" (Jones, Wegner, Bunds, Edwards, & Bocarro, 2018, p. 83). As such, the authors caution that as a multidirectional, non-hierarchical approach, the viability of shared leadership hinges on two key factors: the support available (in terms of resources, knowledge, and skills) and alignment with local culture (the beliefs, norms, and values of the community in question). In the case of Wakefield Youth Sport, such challenges became obvious when a variety of factors was limiting the success of the SFD organisation. From a leadership (development) perspective, these included the volunteer nature of the organisation and the lack of human capital, which resulted in difficulty maintaining interorganisational relationships and exchanges. Moreover, as limited formal training and opportunity for engagement among volunteer networks were available, the shared leadership approach did not result in the desired socio-managerial outcomes. And finally, given that most volunteers were working full time, they had neither the time nor the framework for capacity building and sustainable SFD network building.

The authors of the Wakefield Youth Sport study suggest that when there is a lack of human capital in the community, perhaps a more hierarchical leadership structure is needed until the organisation/community is able to develop its own leaders to operate under a 'shared leadership' framework. As such, they posit that the previously introduced 'servant leadership' approach presents a suitable intermediary method before the final goal of shared leadership can be realised. While the social identity approach (see Chapter 2) has not featured in these analyses of shared leadership, the framework offers some complementary extensions of the literature reviewed here. Specifically, for organisations to 'develop their own leaders' in specific social and cultural contexts, actors require a shared understanding of the group to be led – if they are to achieve social influence. The servant approach – as an interim approach – offers a useful basis to activate such shared understandings. By forfeiting personal interests as a servant leader, the incumbent figure can align their practices with core values and interests of the group. In turn, as group members begin to self-categorise with these meaningful definitions of the group, it provides an empowering frame for shared leadership in which more horizontal leadership practices might be encouraged.

Challenges from the field

Despite the positive uptake and increasing application of servant leadership and shared leadership theory in SFD, scholars have pointed out several challenges in this space. For instance, both theories suggest that the driving desire to be involved is to assist, support, or empower others; hence, a strong sense of personal commitment to the values of the SFD programme is often a primary factor for individuals who become leaders. Fostering these values and making sure leaders (and their followers) do not get emotionally, mentally, or physically 'burned out' is an important consideration when establishing leadership structures. However, servant leadership theory does not specifically feature any core factors that take this consideration into account – according to van Dierendonck (2011), it is a theory that demonstrates what a leader could and should be, but not how to achieve it. A similar argument can be made in the context of Welty Peachey and Burton's (2017) six contributions to servant leadership (outlined earlier). While a follow-up study with an extended author team (Welty Peachey, Burton, Wells, & Chung, 2018) confirmed that servant leadership can indeed support the development of autonomy, competency, and relatedness amongst followers, detail around how to achieve specific benefits remains limited.

Another challenge of servant leadership was previously highlighted by van Dierendonck (2011), who cautioned that there may be a concern about the negative connotation of the word 'servant'. He argued that the term may suggest passivity and indecisiveness and, even more, letting go of power. Managers may therefore dislike the term because it may imply softness and weakness, more appropriate for serving staff than for leaders. In the SFD space, where managers tend to have varied professional backgrounds and where they are often required to serve several roles at once, this may be a problem. For instance, while community sport staff and international development experts are generally trained in socio-managerial development and 'social leadership' skills, the more traditional sport coaches, athletes, and administrators are not. However, the latter hold significant power qua position and/or status – something they *can* use meaningfully as servant leaders, but also something they may *misuse* when applying a more traditional, paternalistic leadership style. In specific cultural contexts – where leadership is portrayed as, and linked with, individual strength and communal power – finding suitably qualified and accepted servant leaders may be particularly challenging.

Next, in the context of international development work, a significant struggle in the wider discussions around SFD leadership exists in often unequal donor-recipient relationships. Many SFD programmes are delivered in low- and middle-income countries (LMICs) or in marginalised social contexts in high-income countries (HICs). These programmes are often initiated, supported, or led by 'cause champions' or external 'change agents' from powerful HICs who are committed to realising positive change (processes) in community contexts. As 'strangers' from outside the community – or even from another region or nation – they may lack the cultural understanding of how to operate in a local context (Phillips & Schulenkorf, 2017; Schulenkorf, 2010). While they may well possess the technical or managerial knowledge to run projects, they are often ill-equipped to meaningfully advise on and/or evaluate SFD initiatives. In extreme cases, externals will employ a dominant, paternalistic, or even a neocolonial view of managing development (Coalter, 2010, 2013; Darnell, 2012; Darnell & Hayhurst, 2011). Consequently, people from LMIC settings may – rightly or otherwise – perceive their own status as less powerful compared to their international HIC partners. In such circumstances, it takes strong shared leaders to bring largely disparate groups onto the same page and to provide a level playing field in which engagement and cooperation can flourish.

Related to this issue, misunderstandings may arise in the local vs. international understanding of the terms 'leadership' and 'leadership development'. For instance, in some cultures, leadership roles are passed on from generation to generation, and they evolve around cultural protocols that are distinct to a particular community. This speaks to a need for contextualised operations of SFD providers, including funders, managers, and evaluators. In cases where a full understanding of the local context is lacking, a clash between outside development workers and local communities is likely to occur with potentially significant negative impacts for the programme and its stakeholders. In such cases, shared leadership will have to involve aspects of reciprocal engagement, learning, and social justice to establish the ethical climate necessary for meaningful operations.

Future (leadership research) opportunities in SFD

Our brief review of servant leadership and shared leadership in the context of SFD has identified a number of challenges for SFD organisations and their partners, as well as related opportunities for future SFD practice and research. First, in this global era, the cross-cultural aspects of servant leadership deserve more attention. Van Dierendonck (2011) has previously suggested that an important focus for future research is to investigate whether servant leadership is more likely to occur in countries with a strong humane orientation and a lower power distance (macro level), or if experiences are indeed more specifically related to individuals and their leadership style (hence, the micro level). Building on this, the extent to which servant leadership is experienced differently across national contexts and within multinational settings deserves to be explored. As discussed, in an SFD setting – where cross-cultural engagement between stakeholders is common and certainly not without controversy – empirical studies on the characteristics of local and international servant leaders are welcome. Adding to those studies could be research that engages in comparative multi-case studies that investigate the strategies and processes employed by different SFD leaders

Case study – sport leadership challenges in Samoa

David Lakisa, UTS Business School

Samoa (formerly Western Samoa), a Pacific Island nation in Polynesia with a current population of approximately 190,000, achieved its independence from New Zealand in 1962. Politically and socioculturally, Samoa is governed by 'fa'asamoa' (the Samoan Way). Fa'asamoa is an integral part of Samoan life, celebrating and embracing values and traditions related to local culture and environment. The central tenets of fa'asamoa include aiga (family), tautala Samoa (Samoan language), gafa (genealogies), matai (chiefly system), lotu (church), and fa'alavelave (ceremonial and other family obligations).

The politics of Samoa take place in a framework of a parliamentary representative democratic state whereby the Prime Minister of Samoa is the head of government. Existing alongside the country's Western-style political system is the fa'amatai chiefly system of sociopolitical governance and organisation. The combination of the two political systems and traditional ways of life bring about opportunities and challenges, and some of them can be evidenced in the management and leadership in sport.

The main sports played in Samoa are Rugby Union, rugby league, and Samoan cricket (kirikiti). Other popular sports are netball, volleyball, and soccer. However, Rugby Union is Samoa's national game, and the 'Manu Samoa' national team captured the world's attention with their success in the 1991 World Cup, where the Samoans performed outstandingly and reached the quarter-finals. Many players – past and present – are considered 'local heroes', and they take leadership roles both within the sporting scene and the wider sociopolitical arena.

A traditional Samoan proverb on leadership states 'Ole ala ile pule ole tautua', meaning 'the pathway to leadership is service'. While Samoan cultural values strongly advocate for the upholding of fa'asamoa, the behaviour of some sport leaders in Samoa – both on and off the field – has fallen well short of public expectation. In particular, issues included:

1   Corruption, fraud, and poor governance
2   Questionable links to political influencers
3   Misallocation of resources
4   Conflicted priorities and mission drift

Some of the leadership dilemmas are linked with professional sport in Samoa – including questionable leadership surrounding Samoan Rugby Union (SRU). Interestingly, the SRU chairman is the Prime Minister of Samoa, Mr Tuilaepa Lupesoliai Sailele Malielegao. Following numerous mismanagement allegations and player protests over the past decade, in November 2017 he announced that the organisation was bankrupt; he even went on to ask the public to donate money to keep the sport alive (Jones, 2017). These claims were strongly denied by the world governing body, World Rugby, who in turn accused SRU of poor governance and financial mismanagement (BBC Sport, 2017). With Rugby Union considered the leader in Samoan sport – and the Prime Minister in charge of its operations – these allegations also play an indirect yet important role in the many SFD programmes in the country.

In regard to SFD, leadership struggles have been evident in regard to the misallocation of resources and conflicted development priorities. As Khoo, Schulenkorf, and Adair (2014) pointed out, Samoa relies heavily upon assistance from foreign countries to finance both sport participation and social development goals. For example, since 2011 there has been targeted funding into Samoa through the Pacific Sport Partnership (PSP) Programme – an Australian Government initiative, funded by the Australian Department of Foreign Affairs and Trade. The PSP intends to facilitate the partnering of Australian national sporting organisations with Pacific counterparts in order to deliver SFD programmes focussed on social development aims. The PSP spans 11 sports and has been implemented across nine Pacific nations (for more detail, see Sherry, Schulenkorf, Seal, Nicholson, & Hoye, 2017). While the focus of the SFD activities is supposed to be placed on social and health-related development outcomes, reports suggest that priority is often given to developing the skill and talent of young players. Especially in Rugby Union the potential for a mission drift regarding SFD delivery is high. Here, SFD leaders are faced with a scenario where participation in an SFD programme is often not about social aspects and educational values, but for many young (male) rugby players it is about 'getting off the island' (Kwauk, 2014). The desire to seek better sporting and living conditions overseas is sparked by global sporting achievements of Samoans, specifically in the US, Europe, or Australia. Across the macro, meso, and micro levels, SFD leadership groups are therefore tasked with avoiding a mission drift and focussing on community development goals – in line with serving local needs and PSP funders' expectations – as well as navigating potentially conflicted priorities of players who mainly engage with professional aspirations in mind.

with the intent of contributing to SFD-specific theoretical frameworks and/or recommendations for best practice around leadership.

In advancing SFD-specific leadership studies, something can be learned from the area of youth sport development where examinations of creating, managing, and leveraging leadership have already been conducted (e.g. Gould & Voelker,

2010; Martinek, Schilling, & Hellison, 2006; Vella, Oades, & Crowe, 2013). In particular, Gould and Voelker (2010) discussed efforts to develop leadership through an educational approach to the sport captaincy experience. In their study they highlighted that sport coaches can play numerous important roles in the process – including those of mentors, teachers, and critical supporters. It seems that sport managers can learn from these experiences; in fact, by adding empirical socio-managerial research, SFD scholars may be able to contribute to the development of strong, inclusive, and well-respected SFD leaders under different leadership types.

Related to this suggestion is an increased focus on connecting SFD leadership with aspects of economic development and the business concept of entrepreneurship in particular. This nexus promises to play an increasingly important role in SFD practice, especially given the challenge of many SFD projects to sustain themselves beyond the time of external funding. Unfortunately, to date, there are a limited number of studies conducted in this space (for a notable exception see Cohen & Welty Peachey, 2015) and, in fact, on the wider topic of building and improving livelihoods through sport overall (see Schulenkorf, Sherry, & Rowe, 2016). This dearth of research is surprising given that financial growth and independence – key aspects of the livelihood concept – play a central part in improving living conditions for (members of) disadvantaged communities (Coalter, 2010; Portes & Landholt, 2000). Therefore, SFD leadership scholars can and should use the opportunity to make the next step in this important field of study. If Step 1 is to understand the relationship between external funders and local communities, then Step 2 requires knowledge that is more specific and insights into the peculiarities of realising business opportunities and leveraging existing community resources – including human and social capital – to secure economic gains without compromising sociocultural values for SFD organisations and communities, and their individual members.

Conclusion

This chapter has focussed on leadership in the context of SFD programmes. Given the significant growth of SFD organisations and projects in recent years, the need for the right kind of leadership approach in this increasingly competitive space is more evident than ever. Similarly, it has become obvious that leadership in the context of SFD – where projects are often orchestrated by local and international stakeholders – is an area of significant importance and potential competitive advantage for people, communities, and organisations. Hence, we need to conduct more applied research to specifically address the peculiarities of leaders and leadership in the complex socio-managerial SFD environment.

This chapter has discussed two of the most relevant leadership theories as they apply to SFD, namely servant leadership and shared leadership. While both these theories are similar in their underpinning approach of helping organisations and communities in efforts towards providing a social service, the core difference is that shared leadership is inherently multidirectional in terms of power structure, while servant leadership is more hierarchical. Depending on the socio-managerial setup and stakeholder context, one may therefore be better suited than the other. While new SFD initiatives may initially need the guidance of a strong servant leader, more established programmes may work well under a shared leadership model that combines many different strengths and assists in maximising capabilities amongst key stakeholders.

Leadership theory and leading in practice are, however, two different things. The Rugby Union case study from Samoa highlights the important and often challenging role of sport leaders in SFD and beyond; moreover, it has alluded to the often complex – and at times conflicting – social, cultural, economic, and political demands leaders have to deal with. Especially in sporting circles, the question may be asked if sport leaders are indeed 'serving' their followers to the best of their ability. Finally, this chapter has listed a number of future opportunities to advance research and practice in SFD leadership. In particular, cross-cultural aspects of leadership are an intriguing space for further research, given the large number of internationally funded but locally implemented SFD projects. Questions around power, influence, and capacity building will continue to play an important role in this space.

References

BBC Sport. (2017, 20 November). Autumn tests: Samoa rugby not bankrupt, says world rugby. Retrieved from https://www.bbc.com/sport/rugby-union/42059958

Burnett, C. (2015). Assessing the sociology of sport: On sport for development and peace. *International Review for the Sociology of Sport, 50*(4–5), 385–390. doi:10.1177/1012690214539695

Coalter, F. (2010). The politics of sport-for-development: Limited focus programmes and broad gauge problems? *International Review for the Sociology of Sport, 45*(3), 295–314. doi:10.1177/1012690210366791

Coalter, F. (2013). *Sport for development: What game are we playing?* Abingdon: Routledge.

Cohen, A., & Welty Peachey, J. (2015). The making of a social entrepreneur: From participant to cause champion within a sport-for-development context. *Sport Management Review, 18*(1), 111–125. doi:10.1016/j.smr.2014.04.002

Darnell, S. (2012). *Sport for development and peace: A critical sociology.* London: A&C Black.

Darnell, S. C., & Black, sD. R. (2011). Mainstreaming sport into international development studies. *Third World Quarterly, 32*(3), 367–378. doi:10.1080/01436597.2011.5 73934

Day, D. V. (2000). Leadership development: A review in context. *The Leadership Quarterly, 11*(4), 581–613. doi:10.1016/S1048-9843(00)00061-8

Edwards, M. B. (2015). The role of sport in community capacity building: An examination of sport for development research and practice. *Sport Management Review, 18*(1), 6–19. doi:10.1016/j.smr.2013.08.008

Gould, D., & Voelker, D. K. (2010). Youth sport leadership development: Leveraging the sports captaincy experience. *Journal of Sport Psychology in Action, 1*(1), 1–14.

Greenleaf, R. K. (1977). *Servant leadership: A journey into the nature of legitimate power and greatness.* New York: Paulist Press.

Jones, C. (2017, 8 November). Autumn tests: Samoa rugby is bankrupt, says country's prime minister. *BBC Sport.* Retrieved from https://www.bbc.com/sport/rugby-union/41915435

Jones, G. J., Wegner, C. E., Bunds, K. S., Edwards, M. B., & Bocarro, J. N. (2018). Examining the environmental characteristics of shared leadership in a sport-for-development organization. *Journal of Sport Management, 32*(2), 82–95. doi:10.1123/jsm.2017-0274

Kang, S., & Svensson, P. G. (2018). Shared leadership in sport for development and peace: A conceptual framework of antecedents and outcomes. *Sport Management Review.* doi:10.1016/j.smr.2018.06.010

Khoo, C., Schulenkorf, N., & Adair, D. (2014). The benefits and limitations of using cricket as a sport for development tool in Samoa. *Cosmopolitan Civil Societies: An Interdisciplinary Journal, 6*(1), 76–102. doi:10.5130/ccs.v6i1.3737

Kwauk, C. (2014). No longer just a past time: Sport for development in times of change. *The Contemporary Pacific, 26*(2), 202–223.

Levermore, R., & Beacom, A. (Eds.). (2009). *Sport and international development.* Basingstoke: Palgrave Macmillan.

Lyras, A., & Welty Peachey, J. (2011). Integrating sport-for-development theory and praxis. *Sport Management Review, 14*(4), 311–326.

Martinek, T., Schilling, T., & Hellison, D. (2006). The development of compassionate and caring leadership among adolescents. *Physical Education & Sport Pedagogy, 11*(2), 141–157.

McCall, M. W. (2010). Recasting leadership development. *Industrial and Organizational Psychology, 3*(1), 3–19. doi:10.1111/j.1754-9434.2009.01189.x

Patterson, K. A. (2003). *Servant leadership: A theoretical model* (PhD), Regent University, Virginia Beach (3082719).

Pearce, C. L., & Conger, J. A. (2003). *Shared leadership: Reframing the hows and whys of leadership.* Thousand Oaks, CA: Sage Publications.

Phillips, P., & Schulenkorf, N. (2017). Coaches, officials, and change agents in sport development. In E. Sherry, N. Schulenkorf, & P. Phillips (Eds.), *Managing sport development: An international approach* (pp. 107–118). New York City: Routledge.

Portes, A., & Landholt, P. (2000). Social capital: Promise and pitfalls of its role in development. *Journal of Latin American Studies, 32*(2), 529–547.

Schulenkorf, N. (2010). The roles and responsibilities of a change agent in sport event development projects. *Sport Management Review, 13*(2), 118–128. doi:10.1016/j.smr.2009.05.001

Schulenkorf, N. (2012). Sustainable community development through sport and events: A conceptual framework for sport-for-development projects. *Sport Management Review, 15*(1), 1–12. doi:10.1016/j.smr.2011.06.001

Schulenkorf, N. (2017). Managing sport-for-development: Reflections and outlook. *Sport Management Review, 20*(3), 143–151. doi:10.1016/j.smr.2016.11.003

Schulenkorf, N., & Adair, D. (2014). Sport-for-development: The emergence and growth of a new genre. In N. Schulenkorf & D. Adair (Eds.), *Global sport-for-development: Critical perspectives* (pp. 3–11). Basingstoke: Palgrave Macmillan.

Schulenkorf, N., Sherry, E., & Rowe, K. (2016). Sport-for-development: An integrated literature review. *Journal of Sport Management, 30*(1), 22–39. doi:10.1123/jsm.2014-0263

Sherry, E., Schulenkorf, N., & Phillips, P. (Eds.). (2016). *Managing sport development: An international approach.* Abingdon: Routledge.

Sherry, E., Schulenkorf, N., Seal, E., Nicholson, M., & Hoye, R. (2017). Sport-for-development in the south pacific region: Macro-, meso-, and micro-perspectives. *Sociology of Sport Journal, 34*(4), 303–316.

van Dierendonck, D. (2011). Servant leadership: A review and synthesis. *Journal of Management, 37*(4), 1228–1261. doi:10.1177/0149206310380462

Vella, S. A., Oades, L. G., & Crowe, T. P. (2013). The relationship between coach leadership, the coach-athlete relationship, team success, and the positive developmental experiences of adolescent soccer players. *Physical Education and Sport Pedagogy, 18*(5), 549–561.

Welty Peachey, J., & Burton, L. (2017). Servant leadership in sport for development and peace: A way forward. *Quest, 69*(1), 125–139. doi:10.1080/00336297.2016.1165123

Welty Peachey, J., Burton, L., Wells, J., & Chung, M. R. (2018). Exploring servant leadership and needs satisfaction in the sport for development and peace context. *Journal of Sport Management, 32*(2), 96–108. doi:10.1123/jsm.2017-0153

8 Leading high performance sport

Introduction

In the four-year lead up to Rio 2016, the Australian Institute of Sport (AIS) invested AU $332 million in the development of high performance athletes (Martino, 2016). In the same cycle, UK Sport spent £355 million (AU $460 million) (Rees et al., 2016). Such high levels of funding are also associated with unprecedented scrutiny and pressures for success. The highly pressurised context of high performance sport (HPS) situates athletes in environments that create competitive (e.g. losing) and organisational stressors (e.g. underfunding) (Fletcher & Hanton, 2003; Thelwell, Weston, Greenlees, & Barnard, 2008). Taken together, the high levels of elite sport funding and the stressful environment in which athletes, coaches, staff, and administrators operate underline *why* leadership plays a crucial role in building HPS success. Yet HPS leadership is a heterogeneous phenomenon that occurs at a variety of levels and through a plethora of roles (more than are discussed in the present literature). Underlining the breadth of HPS leadership, roles that affect its operation span from CEOs of HPS agencies (e.g. UK Sport or Sport Australia) to governing bodies and their boards to national performance directors (NPDs – individuals with the role and responsibility of overseeing the performance outcomes of a whole sport) to coaches and support staff (e.g. strength and conditioning trainers) to athletes. Each of these leadership levels is fundamentally involved in the delivery of HPS outcomes and success. In the following chapter, we review the literature on leadership in HPS from roles with the broadest remit (i.e. setting national elite sport strategy) through to leaders with the most specific involvement in performance (i.e. athletes). In order to introduce and explain leadership in HPS, we:

1 Define HPS and consider what constitutes 'high performance'
2 Discuss the HPS policy agenda and its role in shaping leadership at other levels of sport
3 Articulate the organisational and leadership factors that influence the success of NPDs
4 Investigate the role of coaches as leaders and factors that influence success
5 Discuss horizontal leadership approaches and athletes as leaders.

What is high performance sport?

Although a seemingly straightforward concept, the use of the terms 'elite', 'high performance', and 'expertise' in relation to sport performance are highly inconsistent (Rees et al., 2016; Swann, Moran, & Piggott, 2015). These terms have been used to denote super-elite athletes (i.e. medal winning) through to regional or university level performers. As such, there is confusion over what these terms actually mean. Swann et al. (2015) advance a classification method for the degree to which a performance or performer can be deemed 'expert'. This model considers an:

1   Athlete's highest level of competition
2   His or her success at this level of competition
3   The period of time he or she has competed at the standard
4   The relative competitiveness of the sport in his or her country (i.e. sprinters in the United States move through a far more contested system than their peers in Norway)
5   The intensity of global competition in the activity (i.e. football [soccer] is more globally competitive than Australian Rules Football).

In the present chapter, we provide a broad overview of HPS leaders that operate at various levels of 'eliteness' for a couple of reasons. First, much literature has been written on NPDs, who have a remit to oversee performance pathways for super-elite athletes (Hardy et al., 2017; Rees et al., 2016) and young athletes entering the national talent development pathway (Sotiriadou, 2013). Therefore, ignoring some of this literature would present a limited overview of the NPD leadership role. Second, while the psychological and social functioning of super-elite athletes has been shown to vary from non-medalling high performance athletes (Hardy et al., 2017); there is no evidence that factors underpinning leadership success vary in a similar pattern. As such, we draw on a range of HPS environments in the present chapter to develop a rounded perspective on the leadership of HPS.

The rounded perspective we take in this chapter also reflects that elite sport success is not a simple process but rather the confluence of a range of variables (De Bosscher, De Knop, Van Bottenburg, & Shibli, 2006). To understand leadership in HPS, it is first important to comprehend the complex policy and funding environments that provide an overarching framework for leadership activities. In this regard, De Bosscher et al. (2006) locate the activities that can be influenced by leaders of HPS at the meso (i.e. broader policy context) and micro levels (athlete and coach environment) of the sport system in the nine-pillar model. The first two pillars of the model by De Bosscher et al. (2006) are crucial to successful leadership. First, the funding allocated to HPS in a country is a key predictor of future success. Financial support provides leaders with resources for infrastructure, education, talent identification, coaching, scientific research, and the capacity to translate ambitious visions into reality. Second, countries are more likely to be successful when policy is developed and led in an integrated way at a national level (see further discussion later). Such an approach confers a clear leadership vision from the national performance sport agency (e.g. UK Sport) which, in turn, offers a coherent framework in which NPDs, coaches, and athletes can lead at different levels of their chosen sport.

The cultivation of the different pillars that underpin sporting success (cf. De Bosscher et al., 2006) has also been termed as the creation of 'high performance environments' in which the goal is to create circumstances through which success is 'sustainable' and 'inevitable' (Fletcher & Streeter, 2016; Jones, Gittins, & Hardy, 2009). Within this model, Jones et al. augment the model by De Bosscher et al. (2006), stipulating that at the centre of any successful high performance environment is leadership that sets a clear vision, offers support (cf. Rees & Hardy, 2000), and challenges staff, coaches, and athletes. It is from these central leadership processes that performance enablers (i.e. clear information and incentives) and people (i.e. attitudes, beliefs, and capacity) are ingrained in a culture that fosters high levels of innovation, staff and athlete well-being, achievement, and sound internal processes (Jones et al., 2009). Managing the tensions that the competing nature of these four outcomes creates is a core goal of leadership throughout the leadership levels of HPS. To look more closely at leadership practices at different levels, we begin by discussing the role and function of NPDs.

National performance directors

Operating in relation to specific sports (e.g. swimming), NPDs have become a key focus of sport leadership researchers. Sotiriadou (2013) defines the role of an NPD as an employee who sits below the General Manager or Executive Director of a national governing body (NGB) and reports directly to them in relation to performance. NPDs have roles for staff supervision (e.g. coaches, elite programme coordinators, support staff), which will vary in terms of scope depending on the type of organisation (e.g. the NPDs for Athletics Australia will oversee more athletes than his or her counterpart in the Australian Biathlon Association). While coaches are tasked with leading athlete performance improvements NPDs occupy a more abstract position with responsibility for a far broader range of activities and strategies (Fletcher & Arnold, 2011; Sotiriadou, 2013). As such, occupants have a multifaceted role that is critical to the achievement of success in HPS. Research on NPDs has focussed on:

- Structural and operational issues that can enable leadership success (Arnold, Fletcher, & Molyneux, 2012)
- Facets of NPD leadership success (Arnold, Fletcher, & Molyneux, 2015; Arnold et al., 2012)
- Factors that contribute to new NPDs being able to lead and sustain cultural change (Cruickshank, Collins, & Minten, 2014, 2015)

- The work of NPDs to lead and cultivate a shared identity across coaches, athletes, and support staff (Slater, Barker, Coffee, & Jones, 2015; Slater, Evans, & Barker, 2013).

Prior to considering factors leading to success, it is important to consider the organisational circumstances in which NPDs *are more likely to be successful*. Arnold et al. (2012) conducted a qualitative study with existing NPDs in order to establish the organisational circumstances that underpin successful leadership. The NPDs in their sample argued for five main areas of organisational action that were *supportive* of leader success. First, the individual that assumes the role of NPD is important. Therefore, as a first step, national sport organisations (NSOs) need to engage in a thorough process of recruitment that seeks to match the task and role responsibilities of the job to the most suitable candidate. Second, on assuming the position of NPD, there is a need for the employer to adopt a set of policies and processes that minimise top-down interference and give the NPD scope to execute their role. Third, to create alignment between the vision of the NPD and the organisation, there is a need for structures and systems that are supportive of key objectives. For example, this may include appropriate funding for athletes, coaches, support staff, and facilities. Such support ensures an environment in which the NPD can focus on the minutiae of their role, rather than concerns over, for example, athlete income. Fourth, NPDs benefit from employment in inclusive organisations. The development of strong cultures within NSOs provides NPDs with a strong platform from which to execute their role. In organisations with weak cultures, it is harder for NPDs to create a sense of coherence and purpose that creates issues in the development of HPS success. Finally, noting the four-year cycles familiar to most Olympic sports, Arnold et al. (2012) argue that more temporal and long-term approaches that are less tied to Olympic cycles and short-term success would allow NPDs to lead in a more pragmatic manner.

Moving to consider the NPD role, Arnold et al. (2012) and Fletcher and Arnold (2011) offer recommendations for leader success. Initially, Arnold et al. (2012) articulate the need for successful NPDs to establish clear role definitions and responsibilities for the members of their team. This leadership step is crucial as it creates clear guidelines stipulating who is responsible for tasks and timelines for completion. Not only does this enhance NPD success – it is also linked to broader benefits, such as work-life balance, team atmosphere, and productivity (Arnold et al., 2012). To supplement this process, NPDs should also seek to develop strong relationships with people inside and outside of the organisation. In both of these activities, the NPD is seeking to foster communication, teamwork, and cohesion that are conducive to internal success as well as the nourishment of important relationships with NPDs and staff in other sports, and stakeholders operating at higher levels of sports governing structures in order to transfer and obtain knowledge, and strengthen networks (e.g. UK Sport).

In a recent example of this process, Cricket Australia embarked on a ten-day tour of the United States to learn about new and different leadership practices in the National Football League, Major League Baseball, and Golf (Burnett, 2018). Through relationships with international agencies, Cricket Australia designed a trip that aligned with a culture of learning, instilled from the CEO, through the NPD, Head Coach, and Captain. In doing so, James Sutherland (CEO), Pat Howard (NPD), Justin Langer (Head Coach), and Tim Paine (Captain) set out to learn as well as develop a more harmonious relationship between key leaders in Cricket Australia to strengthen culture moving forward.

Successful NPDs also need to be aware of the situation and context in which they lead. For example, an NPD in gymnastics may work with high performance athletes who are far younger than those in other activities (e.g. athletics). As such, the age of participants may render certain leadership approaches useful in some circumstances and unsuitable in others. In addition, the culture of the sport an NPD leads is also an important concern. Skilful NPDs should tailor advice and leadership content so that it aligns with the sport culture in order to enhance the chances of buy-in from athletes, coaches, and support staff. Cruickshank et al. (2014) studied new performance directors (PDs) with a view to understanding how they could achieve cultural change when new to the role. They found that the contextual circumstances that new PDs encountered on incumbency occurred at different levels. At the macro level, PDs had to contend with history, traditions, and other long-established features of the sport. In short, there are 'accepted ways of doing things' in some sports that new PDs need to consider on assuming their role. Meso level considerations reflect the position of the sport in relation to others in terms of popularity, status, or funding. At the micro level cultural concerns derived from stakeholder perceptions and scrutiny created cultural pressures for new PDs.

It is within these frameworks of culture that PDs sought to lead and achieve success in HPS. Cruickshank et al. (2014) observed a process whereby the PD in their qualitative sample constantly made efforts to "link all performance-based systems, structures, processes, actions, and discourses to the new and/or refined social norms" (p. 117). In this sense, Cruickshank et al. argue that checklist approaches to developing and enriching culture in organisations are flawed and short-sighted. Rather than seeing culture as a static property, therefore, they advocate for the treatment of culture as a dynamic construct with no specific "end point". Therefore, in a similar vein to the social identity approach discussed in Chapter 2, NPDs are entrepreneurs that need to be perpetually aware of the shifting situational and contextual dynamics that affect their role.

The entrepreneurial activities of NPDs have received attention from researchers using the social identity approach (Slater et al., 2013, 2015). Slater et al. (2013) analysed the actions and communications used by Sir David Brailsford (Brailsford from hereon) in order to cultivate a positively distinct identity for British Cycling. Specifically, their analysis demonstrated how Brailsford communicated features of the in-group, such as attention to detail, innovation, and a resilience associated with Britishness, each of which Slater et al. argue sought to accentuate similarities between members of British

Cycling and differences in relation to key competitors. The purpose of such communications is the creation of distinctive content that provides athletes, coaches, and support staff with a source of shared identity. In a broader study of leader media behaviour during the London 2012 Olympic Games (London 2012 hereon), Slater et al. (2015) discussed the temporal nature of entrepreneurial leader communications. Rather than communicating a static and repeated message through the games, Team Great Britain (GB) leaders developed messages – delivered through a variety of media – that sought to establish the high performance credentials of the group in a continual and evolving manner prior to, during, and following London 2012. In both studies, Slater and his colleagues emphasise the actions of NPDs in using the media to cultivate a shared identity.

Coach-athlete leadership

The leadership of athletes by coaches presents a series of different challenges. While NPDs are responsible for a broad remit in many cases, coaches and athletes work in closer proximity, and, as such, relationships at this level have been the focus of much attention (Jowett & Chaundy, 2004; Jowett & Cockerill, 2003). While distinct from leadership, we discuss the coach-athlete relationship in this section alongside other factors that researchers have found to enhance or diminish the capacity of an individual to exert legitimate social influence over an individual or group. These factors include sources of organisational stress attributable to leadership (Thelwell et al., 2008), preferred leadership behaviours (Côté & Sedgwick, 2003; Høigaard, Jones, & Peters, 2008), the emotional intelligence of the coach-leader (Chan & Mallett, 2011), player ability and pastoral responsibilities (Thelwell et al., 2008), and athlete narcissism (Arthur, Woodman, Ong, Hardy, & Ntoumanis, 2011).

To lead effectively, coaches need to foster a healthy relationship with athletes (Jowett & Chaundy, 2004; Jowett & Cockerill, 2003). While related to leadership, Jowett and Chaundy (2004) found that leading and having a strong relationship with athletes were distinct. Jowett and Chaundy demonstrate that strong leadership is a key factor leading to task and social cohesion. However, in their study, a strong coach-athlete relationship enhanced leader efficacy and explained more variance in task and group cohesion. As a foundation point, it is crucial for high performance coaches (HPCs) to lead *as well as* forming healthy, bi-directional relationships with the athletes for whom they have responsibility. The coach-athlete relationship is considered a social phenomenon and is described as "a situation (or a process) in which a coach's and an athlete's cognitions, feelings, and behaviors are mutually and causally interrelated" (Jowett & Ntoumanis, 2004, p. 245). Therefore, while leadership without positive relationships may occur (e.g. Jess Varnish and British Cycling) a functional coach-athlete relationship adds to leadership effectiveness (Jowett & Chaundy, 2004) and helps to reduce a major source of stress on the coach (Thelwell et al., 2008) and athlete.

The experience of stress and anxiety are major issues for HPCs (Thelwell et al., 2008). In a comprehensive study of HPC, Thelwell et al. explore the different parts of the coach role that create stress. In relation to leadership, three themes emerged: organisation, other coaches, and athletes. Sport in general (Shilbury, Quick, Westerbeek, Funk, & Karg, 2014) and HPS specifically are dynamic and turbulent environments, both of which create a range of difficult scenarios for coaches. The first source of stress concerns changes that occur at higher organisational levels. For example, the recruitment of a new NPD in HPS would have implications for some coaches, as would the recruitment of a new Chairman in an elite sports club. Therefore, as NPDs need to develop strong cultures and inclusive environments, they also need to develop healthy relationships with the coaches that are delivering *their* strategy. The second source of stress emerges from mixed communications occurring because of athletes working with more than one coach. For example, coach-leaders described experiencing stress when another coach[es] contradicted or confused information they had disseminated to an athlete. Thus, contradictory communications from different can reduce coach-leader effectiveness if there are different understandings of '*correct practices*'. The third source of stress concerned working with athletes of different levels. When coaches worked with a range of athletes with a variety of performance backgrounds, it led to a reduction in leader efficacy. In such situations, coaches deviated from their HPC role because of an enhanced requirement to provide pastoral support.

Côté and Sedgwick (2003) conducted a qualitative study with coaches and athletes to unearth characteristics of successful coach-leaders in rowing. In this study, Côté and Sedgwick argue that HPC need to:

- Set clear plans
- Cultivate a training environment based on positive situations and experiences
- Engage in a clear process of setting goals with athletes
- Implement processes and actions to develop athlete self-confidence
- Display mastery in teaching the core skills associated with the activity
- Cater to the differences that exist between athletes
- Establish a rapport and relationship with each individual athlete.

Høigaard et al. (2008) developed Côté and Sedgwick's work, arguing that the roles played by athletes in teams created additional nuances for coaches. For example, there are important differences between players and substitutes. Adding further complexity to the coach-leader role, these differences are also contingent on team results in matches. When a team is successful, there is a tendency for substitutes or unused players to lack any feeling of personal contribution to the team. As such, successful coaches should pay particular attention to celebrating the contributions of substitutes or unused players through positive feedback after team victories. After losing a match, instead of focussing attention on the players that took the field, successful coach-leaders should empower substitute and unused players in a democratic process of understanding the next steps to arrest the negative performance. This point is supported by Ronglan's (2007) ethnographic findings, which show how important player involvement in evaluation of team performances can be in cultivating perceptions of collective effectiveness.

To this point, we have discussed the importance of HPCs being able to lead and cultivate relationships, reduce stress, manage individuals, set goals, develop confidence, and adapt behaviour to situational cues (e.g. losing). All of this suggests that successful HPCs retain a high level of emotional intelligence. Chan and Mallett (2011) explore this concept in HPCs, noting the importance of this psychological skill in fostering strong coach-athlete relationships. They note that while there are examples of coaches that clearly lack emotional intelligence, it appears to be a critical skill in the development of trust and inspirational environments that are conducive to HPS success (see also Côté & Sedgwick, 2003). This perspective acknowledges the importance of managing 'individuals' as well as groups.

Emphasising the capacity to manage individuals, Arthur et al. (2011) explore how levels of athlete narcissism in HPS affect coach-leader behaviours. Using a transformational approach to leadership Arthur et al. found that narcissistic athletes were less likely to see group goals and teamwork as important. Specifically, the pursuit of group goals is problematic for narcissistic athletes because it reduces focus on their own interests in favour of the greater good of the team. As such, coaches trying to lead athletes who score highly on narcissistic traits – especially in high performance team sports – have a complex task of developing an adherence to group culture and norms. In addition, transformational coach behaviours – such as instilling high performance expectations – were less effective for athletes reporting high narcissistic traits. Therefore, in addition to 'managing individuals' Arthur et al. contribute important information about how the narcissistic tendencies of some athletes create additional challenges for the coach-leader.

Athletes and leadership groups

The most specific form of leadership we discuss in this chapter concerns more horizontal athlete-led behaviours that can have profound influences on performance. Rather than seeing the leadership environment in HPS as the sole domain of coaches, some authors have investigated how athlete leaders can contribute to team effectiveness (e.g. Fransen et al., 2017). This work eschews the dominant top-down approach to leadership in HPS in favour of approaches that empower athletes as leaders. This approach acknowledges that interpersonal (Evans, Eys, & Wolf, 2013; Ronglan, 2007) and group-based dynamics (Fransen et al., 2017) are crucial to team and group success.

Fransen et al. (2017) studied three professional Australian sport teams (one from the National Rugby League and two from the Australian Football League) to explore the relationship between athlete leadership and team effectiveness. The study advanced four main findings that emerged from observing the strength of leadership groups (i.e. up to five players charged with being 'team leaders'). First, in teams that had effective leadership groups, players had a stronger understanding of the common purpose of the group. Second, as proposed by the social identity approach, when social identity is salient and meaningful, team members will invest time and energy to achieve group goals. Third, teams with stronger leadership groups also tended to feature players that were more confident in the collective strength of the group. Finally, strong leadership groups were associated with players offering social support to one another, which was conducive to player improvement. All of these findings were analysed in relation to the social identity approach and provide strong support for the theoretical analysis we provided in Chapter 2. Furthermore, the findings of the study by Fransen et al. (2017) provide compelling support for the importance of developing empowered player leadership groups that play a supplemental function to higher levels of leadership.

Also analysing group-based effectiveness, Evans et al. (2013) explore interpersonal influences that have a shaping effect on success in individual sports. While group cohesiveness is a somewhat obvious imperative in team sport contexts, individual sports (e.g. Triathlon) – at a superficial level – have less of a requirement for shared purpose, etc. However, Evans et al. (2013) observed a series of important interpersonal and group influences that enabled performance. Furthermore, these dynamics bring together the different levels of leadership we have discussed in this chapter. Initially, Evans et al. (2013) show that the groups surrounding HPS environments are shaped by NPDs, nourished by coaches, and shared by athletes. When the broader group is important to an athlete (e.g. Team GB Triathlon), it provides a *meaningful* reason to compete in their individual pursuit *under the banner of a broader identity* involved in contests with rival groups. In addition, interactions with other athletes provide a source of motivation and competition, which lead individual athletes to push themselves harder in order to keep up with other team members. Evans et al. also acknowledge the importance of collective strategies in individual sport. For example, in endurance sports, such as cycling, riders – while competing individually – belong to teams, which cooperate in order to ensure that their 'lead rider' or 'team' is successful (e.g. Team Sky in the Tour de France). As such, although technically an individual sport, the cooperation between teammates creates considerable advantages for individual and collective performance. Finally, shared interpersonal influences create a strong sense of social support for individuals, which can enable elite athletes to cope in stressful periods. Taken together, these findings illustrate that interpersonal and group influences are also important in individual sport. However, Evans et al. (2013) explain that the importance of interpersonal relations and groupness is not constant but becomes more or less salient depending on the contextual features of the athlete environment. Therefore, it is important for NPDs and coaches to cultivate high performance environments that give athletes the opportunity to realise the collective benefits of interpersonal influence *when it is required*.

Case study – British Swimming

Fletcher and Streeter (2016) provide a useful case study of the high performance environment of British Swimming. It offers a useful point of reference to consider how leadership practices across different organisational levels combine, contrast, and – ultimately – underpin success. The first full-time coach of British Swimming was appointed at the end of the 1980s. Emphasising much that we have discussed in this chapter, Fletcher and Streeter (2016) articulate how a crucial transition in the high performance culture in British Swimming emerged that united coaches and swimmers behind a "vision of fast swimming" (p. 129). Arriving at a shared purpose is a crucial step in cultivating groups that can be led successfully (e.g. Arnold et al., 2012). Emphasising the interrelatedness of athletes in a mainly individualistic pursuit (excluding relays) Fletcher and Streeter discuss how a sense of shared ownership and leadership took over from a culture in which individuals were all important. This example portrays an environment that actively sought to mitigate the issues that Arthur et al. (2011) observed in relation to athlete narcissism in favour of an environment that prioritised collective goals and the empowerment of leaders at NPD, coach, and athlete levels.

Although British Swimming encouraged leadership throughout its ranks, Fletcher and Streeter (2016) argue that this resulted from a vision cultivated by the NPD. This aspect of the British Swimming culture presents a couple of key takeaways from this chapter. First, while athletes and coaches are important leaders in some contexts (e.g. Fransen et al., 2017), the capacity for leaders to emerge at different levels (i.e. coaches and athletes) is enhanced when there is a clear unifying vision. In turn, this shared purpose directs the energies of multiple leaders (e.g. NPDs, coaches, and athletes) in a direction that is conducive to achieving group objectives. This resonates with the social identity approach and the necessity for leaders to engage followers in a culture that has meaning for their self-concept. Second, it offers insight into the pitfalls of athlete empowerment in environments *before* a clear vision has been articulated, established, and ingrained. In instances where coaches and athletes are empowered to lead prior to the establishment of a clear vision, there is a strong possibility of competing agendas, schisms, and confusion, all of which act as a source of stress for coaches and athletes (Thelwell et al., 2008).

Conclusion

In this chapter, we have discussed three levels of leadership that have a crucial influence on HPS. Broadly, the literature we have drawn upon suggests that there is a need for leadership and collaboration from the policy level through the governing bodies of sports through NPDs, coaches, and athletes. Although typically using a top-down approach to the issue of leadership, there is an emerging agenda drawing on the social identity approach that acknowledges the importance of fostering the horizontal dimensions of leadership as well. Regardless of approach, leaders at all levels of sport have a clear need to set a common purpose, to create a sense that group members share and see value in the common purpose, and cultivate inclusive environments that allow strong relationships and communication networks to develop.

Case study – High performance leadership and the Geelong Football Club

Lewis Whales, UTS Business School

Geelong Football Club provides an interesting example of effective multilevel club leadership, which turned around the club's fortunes – and organisational success – between 1999 and 2009. This time frame marked a significant turnround for the club both on and off the field. This case looks at the leadership contributions of four individuals that occupied positions at different levels of the organisation: Frank Costa, Brian Cook, Mark Thompson, and Tom Harley. These four men were all at the Geelong Football Club during the 1999–2009 period and held key leadership roles. Frank Costa was appointed the president of the club prior to 1999 and continued in the role beyond 2009. Brian Cook was appointed CEO of the club in 1999 and remains in the position. Mark Thompson was appointed the senior coach of the club prior to 2000 and remained beyond 2009, and Tom Harley was appointed captain of the club for the 2007 season, retiring at the end of 2009 (Geelong Football Club, 2009; Harley, 2010).

On the field in 1999, Geelong Football Club finished 11th in the 16-team competition, while off-field they were approximately AU $10 million in debt. This was quickly improved with a merger in 1999 of the Geelong Football Social Club and Geelong Football Club Limited. As a result, Geelong's net assets was AU $714,758. During the mid- to late 1990s the Geelong Football Club was also in the midst of a cultural crisis, with the club, the fans, and the players not knowing what they stood for (Cook, 2017). Geelong did not experience on-field success until 2007. Geelong won the minor premiership by a margin of three games, triumphed in the Grand Final by a record margin, and nine players were selected for All Australian honours. In 2008, Geelong only lost one game before they ultimately fell short in the Grand Final. They bounced back in 2009 from second place to win the Grand Final. In addition to winning the AFL premiership in 2009 the Geelong Football Club had also reached AU $8,645,003 in net assets, AU $7,930,245 more than 1999 (Cook, 2017;

Geelong Football Club Limited, 2009). This turnround did not occur by accident but rather was the outcome of clear and proactive leadership that flowed through the club.

The first indication of success under the new leadership regime was the cultural turnround experienced at Geelong during the early 2000s, initiated by Frank Costa and continued by Brian Cook (Cook, 2017). Costa undertook three key actions: appointing a new board; personally guaranteeing against loans (to ensure the financial viability of the club) (Niall, 2007); and hiring as CEO Brian Cook, who many considered to be the best administrator in the game (Griffin, 2016). What attracted Cook to Geelong from West Coast Eagles was the character-first view held by Costa. Inspired by this vision Cook first developed the club's mission, vision, values, and strategies through workshops with important stakeholders. This challenged the status quo at Geelong, with 80% of staff leaving in Cook's first two years, presenting the opportunity to replace them with values-first leaders. The values identified by Cook from the stakeholder workshops in 1999 were respect, excellence, innovation, strong work ethic, teamwork, and customer service (Cook, 2017). Further to values-driven human resource practices, difficult and bold financial moves had to be made as well. Geelong asked long-term sponsors to make payments upfront and sold their significant debt to the Bendigo Bank in order to meet short-term obligations. Stadium plans were put in place to improve the club's long-term viability.

In 2005, the Geelong values evolved to respect, precision, adventurous, conviction, and unity through inclusion and consideration (Cook, 2017). A key early appointment of Cook's was Mark Thompson as coach; he was said to be a coach who valued players and his coaching staff, and created unity between the players and the administration of the club, making players feel secure and connected to the Geelong Football Club (Fjeldstad, 2012). Although the setting of abstract organisational values set a clear vision for the club, Thompson had the more specific job of getting players and coaches to buy in to the new vision. The final piece of the club's leadership puzzle was the 2007 appointment of Tom Harley as captain. Harley was somewhat of a pioneer as he was not a star player; however he was a standout at representing the club's values. In this sense, he embodied the features of the club that were most important. This was crucial as it enabled Harley to seek support from other players as leaders and enabled Harley to lead the team in a way that was congruent with the team values. In this sense, Harley was a key leader in terms of creating horizontal support between players for the club values determined by Costa, Cook, and Thompson. This was best demonstrated when the leadership group gave star player Steve Johnson a five-game suspension for an alcohol-related incident during the 2007 preseason (Harley, 2010). According to Brian

Continued

Cook (2017) the Geelong Football Club has built its competitive advantage on great people that fit the Geelong values, great leadership, great plans, and great culture.

Since 2000, the Geelong Cats have won three premierships, finishing in the top eight 14 times, including an eight-year finals streak between 2007 and 2014, and finishing in the top four ten times.

References

Arnold, R., Fletcher, D., & Anderson, R. (2015). Leadership and management in elite sport: Factors perceived to influence performance. *International Journal of Sports Science & Coaching, 10*, 285–304.

Arnold, R., Fletcher, D., & Molyneux, L. (2012). Performance leadership and management in elite sport: Recommendations, advice and suggestions from national performance directors. *European Sport Management Quarterly, 12*, 317–336.

Arthur, C., Woodman, T., Ong, C., Hardy, L., & Ntoumanis, N. (2011). The role of athlete narcissism in moderating the relationship between coaches' transformational leader behaviors and athlete motivation. *Journal of Sport and Exercise Psychology, 33*, 3–19.

Burnett, A. (2018). Langer, Paine set for leadership tour in US [WWW Document]. Cricket.com.au. Retrieved from https://www.cricket.com.au/news/tim-paine-justin-langer-leadership-tour-usa-james-sutherland-pat-howard-captaincy-australia-cricket/2018-08-15 (accessed 29 August 2018).

Chan, J., & Mallett, C. (2011). The value of emotional intelligence for high performance coaching. *International Journal of Sports Science & Coaching, 6*, 315–328.

Cook, B. (2017). 'CEO Geelong Football Club Presentation', *St Joseph's Dinner Presentation*, St Joseph's College Geelong.

Côté, J., & Sedgwick, W. (2003). Effective behaviors of expert rowing coaches: A qualitative investigation of Canadian athletes and coaches. *International Sports Journal, 7*, 62–77.

Cruickshank, A., Collins, D., & Minten, S. (2014). Driving and sustaining culture change in Olympic sport performance teams: A first exploration and grounded theory. *International Journal of Sport and Exercise Psychology, 36*, 107–120.

Cruickshank, A., Collins, D., & Minten, S. (2015). Driving and sustaining culture change in professional sport performance teams: A grounded theory. *Sport, Exercise, and Performance Psychology, 20*, 40–50.

De Bosscher, V., De Knop, P., Van Bottenburg, M., & Shibli, S. (2006). A conceptual framework for analysing sports policy factors leading to international sporting success. *European Sport Management Quarterly, 6*, 185–215.

Evans, B., Eys, M., & Wolf, S. (2013). Exploring the nature of interpersonal influence in elite individual sport teams. *Journal of Applied Sport Psychology, 25*, 448–462.

Fjeldstad, J. (2012). 'Geelong using greatness to create leaders', *Sunday Mail*, 14 October 2012.

Fletcher, D., & Arnold, R. (2011). A qualitative study of performance leadership and management in elite sport. *Journal of Applied Sport Psychology, 23*, 223–242.

Fletcher, D., & Hanton, S. (2003). Sources of organizational stress in elite sports performers. *Sport Psychology, 17*, 175–195.

Fletcher, D., & Streeter, A. (2016). A case study analysis of a high performance environment in elite swimming. *Journal of Organizational Change Management, 16,* 123–141.

Fransen, K., Haslam, A., Mallett, C., Steffens, N., Peters, K., & Boen, F. (2017). Is perceived athlete leadership quality related to team effectiveness? A comparison of three professional sports teams. *Journal of Science and Medicine in Sport, 20,* 800–806.

Geelong Football Club Limited (2009). *Geelong football club concise financial report.* Geelong Football Club, Geelong, Victoria, Australia.

Griffin, N. P. (2016). 'Geelong cats CEO Brian Cook: Character over talent', *The Australian Business Executive,* 17 August 2016.

Hardy, L., Barlow, M., Evans, L., Rees, T., Woodman, T., & Warr, C. (2017). Great British medalists: Psychosocial biographies of super-elite and elite athletes from Olympic sports. *Progress in Brain Research,* 1–119.

Harley, T. (2010). *Standing tall: Confidence, teamwork and learning to lead.* Melbourne: Penguin Books.

Høigaard, R., Jones, G., & Peters, D. (2008). Preferred coach leadership behaviour in elite soccer in relation to success and failure. *International Journal of Sports Science and Coaching, 3*(2), 241–250.

Jones, G., Gittins, M., & Hardy, L. (2009). Creating an environment where high performance is inevitable and sustainable: The high performance environment model. *Annual Review of High Performance Coaching and Consulting, 1,* 139–148.

Jowett, S., & Chaundy, V. (2004). An investigation into the impact of coach leadership and coach-athlete relationship on group cohesion. *Group Dynamics: Theory, Research, and Practice, 8,* 302–311.

Jowett, S., & Cockerill, I. (2003). Olympic medallists' perspective of the athlete–coach relationship. *Sport, Exercise, and Performance Psychology, 4,* 313–331.

Jowett, S., & Ntoumanis, N. (2004). The coach–athlete relationship questionnaire (CART-Q): Development and initial validation. *Scandinavian Journal of Medicine & Science in Sports, 14,* 245–257.

Martino, M. (2016). Rio 2016: Which Olympic sports gave the taxpayer more bang for their buck? *Australian Broadcasting Corporation.* https://www.abc.net.au/news/2016-08-22/rio-olympics-2016-how-much-does-a-medal-cost-taxpayer/7748946

Niall, J. (2007). 'Geelong's nine-year journey', *Brisbane Times,* 27 September 2007.

Rees, T., & Hardy, L. (2000). An investigation of the social support experiences of high-level sports performers. *The Sport Psychologist, 14,* 327–347.

Rees, T., Hardy, L., Güllich, A., Abernethy, B., Côté, J., Woodman, T., … Beccarini, C. (2016). The Great British medalists project: A review of current knowledge on the development of the world's best sporting talent. *Sports Medicine, 46,* 1041–1058.

Ronglan, L. (2007). Building and communicating collective efficacy: A season-long in-depth study of an elite sport team. *Sport Psychology, 21,* 78–93.

Shilbury, D., Quick, S., Westerbeek, H., Funk, D., & Karg, A. (2014). *Strategic sport marketing.* Crows Nest: Allen & Unwin.

Slater, M., Barker, J., Coffee, P., & Jones, M. (2015). Leading for gold: Social identity leadership processes at the London 2012 Olympic Games. *Qualitative Research in Sport, Exercise and Health, 7,* 192–209.

Slater, M., Evans, A., & Barker, J. (2013). Using social identities to motivate athletes towards peak performance at the London 2012 Olympic Games: Reflecting for Rio 2016. *Reflective Practice, 14,* 672–679.

Sotiriadou, P. (2013). The roles of high performance directors within national sporting organizations. In P. Sotiriadou & V. De Bosscher (Eds.), *Managing high performance sport* (pp. 33–46). London: Routledge.

Swann, C., Moran, A., & Piggott, D. (2015). Defining elite athletes: Issues in the study of expert performance in sport psychology. *Sport, Exercise, and Performance Psychology, 16*, 3–14.

Thelwell, R., Weston, N., Greenlees, I., & Barnard, N. (2008). Stressors in elite sport: A coach perspective. *Journal of Sports Sciences, 26*, 905–918.

9 Failed leadership and professional sport
The case of #Sandpapergate

Introduction

Given the vast amount of academic literature that has explored the concept of leadership over the past century, it is surprising how few studies have actually explored leadership failures in any significant depth. The existing literature has mainly examined leadership failure in the context of quantifiable measures such as the impact on an organisation's financial performance (Liu, 2010). Given that the past four decades have been rife with corruption and scandal, both in the field of professional sport and the corporate sector (i.e. Enron), a deeper examination of leadership failure is warranted. Moreover, with the intense and global nature of professional sport, and the wide media attention it garners, the scrutiny of leaders in sport has never been so great, making rigorous academic analysis vital to further our knowledge and our understanding (Katz, 2001). The express aim of this chapter, therefore, is to explore failed leadership, and to do this we use the context of one of the biggest scandals to impact the sport of cricket, otherwise known as #Sandpapergate.

While cheating in sport is not a new (or unusual) phenomenon, it is rarely viewed by the broadcaster's cameras, via the big screen, for all viewers to see in absolute 'crystal' clear detail. This was the unfortunate event that happened to the Australian men's cricket team when the cameras showed Australian fielder Cameron Bancroft using a piece of bright yellow sandpaper to scratch the surface of the red leather cricket ball. The purpose of this action was to get the ball swinging (late) through the air when bowled in order to make it much more difficult for the opposing team's batsmen to hit – this process in cricket is also known as 'reverse swing'.

To make this incident even worse for both the fielder and the Australian team, Bancroft tried to hide the sandpaper down the front of his pants: the television cameras caught all of this and replayed it continuously in slow motion, both on the big screen at the game and via the television broadcast. The ramifications of this incident were enormous for the three players who admitted their involvement, and for the coach of the team, Darren Lehman, who announced his resignation a week later. What made matters even worse for the Australian cricket team was the fact that the other two players involved in sanctioning this cheating included the Captain (Steven Smith) and the Vice-Captain (David Warner).

After a quick investigation, both Smith and Warner were suspended from playing international cricket for 12 months while the more inexperienced test player Bancroft received a nine-month suspension.

In addition to the suspension of three players and the resignation of the coach, the scandal played a significant part in the resignation of the CEO, James Sutherland; the Director of High Performance, Pat Howard; and the President of Cricket Australia, David Peever. As outlined in an independent report commissioned by Cricket Australia that was undertaken by The Ethics Centre (2018) and published in October 2018:

> The leadership of Cricket Australia also accept responsibility for its inadvertent (but foreseeable) failure to create and support a culture in which the will-to-win was balanced by an equal commitment to moral courage and ethical restraint. While good intentions might reduce culpability – they do not lessen responsibility … especially not for those who voluntarily take on the mantle of leadership.
>
> (p. 7)

Theoretical perspectives

As alluded to throughout this book, studies of leadership in the field of sport management have been growing steadily over the past decade (Peachey et al., 2015). This has been highlighted recently by a special issue of the *Journal of Sport Management*, exploring a variety of leadership theories in a sport management context. Leadership studies in a sport management setting have examined the concept of transformational leadership; gender and leadership roles; shared leadership; and, more recently, the crucial area of experience-based leadership development (Frawley, Favaloro, & Schulenkorf, 2018). What is missing in the broader sport management literature is a close examination of failed leadership and the consequences for individuals and organisations of such failure.

The work of Liu (2010) informs this chapter by applying a typology of leadership failure through which to analyse the #Sandpapergate scandal. Liu (2010) has suggested that failed leadership can be viewed from five distinct but interrelated frames. These frames include the framer (whether that be the leader or other parties such as stakeholders), blame (attributed or not attributed), affect (positive or negative), consistency (consistent or inconsistent), and negotiation (complementary or contradictory). By deploying this typology, it is hoped that the analysis of failed leadership will move beyond the use of apologies and the laying of blame to provide a more nuanced view of how leaders frame and are framed by their failures.

Case method

To achieve the stated aim of this chapter the case study deploys media content analysis, which is regarded as a sub-component of the broader research methodology known simply as content analysis (Macnamara, 2005). Content analysis can be described as a "primary messaged centred methodology" (Neundorf,

2002, p. 9) while media content analysis is focussed on "who says what, through which channel, to whom, with what effect" (Lasswell, 1948, p. 12). Media content analysis has been used to examine both news articles published on #Sandpapergate in the main Australian newspapers such as *The Australian, The Age, The Sydney Morning Herald*, and *The Australian Financial Review*. In addition to the content analysis, tweets published that used the aforementioned hashtag were collated and analysed. Keywords such as leadership, governance, cheating, failure, and associated terms were used in the search.

Failed leadership

According to Grint (2001), leadership is an objective social construct that can be evaluated as authentic or inauthentic. Leadership can be moulded by leaders or followers and facilitated through intermediaries such as the media (Liu, 2010). Authentic leadership as a concept has attracted a great deal of interest from management researchers over recent times due to the mounting ethical challenges and pressures organisations and their leaders have faced largely due to increasing public scrutiny and awareness (Eagly, 2005). This pressure has been compounded by the endless access to information and data available through social media platforms. Furthermore, the coverage of corporate and political scandals has intensified through the traditional media with much focus on the ethical wrongdoing by high-profile business leaders and politicians (Liu, 2010).

One response by business and organisation leaders to such public outcry has been that of impression management and therefore image building. This method sees leaders engage in tactics that promote their levels or (image) of competency and attempts to inspire followers to pursue their stated vision. Research in this area has revealed that effective impression management is said to be displayed by leaders when they acknowledge past failure/s, they demonstrate genuine repentance, and they outline a desire to rectify the mistakes they have made (Kusy & Essex, 2007; Tucker, Turner, Barling, Reid, & Elving, 2006).

According to Shamir, Dayan-Horesh, and Adler (2005), exemplification of when leaders recount previous failures and demonstrate perseverance earns not only self respect but also respect from others. Contrastingly, studies have also revealed examples of unsuccessful impression management where the apologies of leaders were seen to be insincere by sophisticated viewers and resulted in the leaders being thought of as weak and incompetent (Liu, 2010; Kusy & Essex, 2007).

Blame framing

Framing of blame is subjective to the leader in what they perceive to be mistakes or failures. Such ideals to framing failure can either detract or enhance a positive presentation of their effectiveness and associated public image/s (Liu, 2010; Fairhurst, 2007). Positive framing of blame that demonstrates courage includes admitting to personal weaknesses, placing blame, and offering an apology (Goffee & Jones, 2001; Kellerman, 2006).

The 'system network of failure framing' framework constructed by Liu (2010) presents leaders with options in how they can actively construct and negotiate their leadership image. As outlined earlier, Liu (2010) argues that failure framing comprises five key elements: the framer, blame, affect, consistency, and negotiation. For the purpose of this analysis, exploration of blame is the central focus of the analysis.

The characteristic of blame in this instance is offered as an explanation of why and/or how leadership failure occurred. The framework breaks failure down into "not attributed" and "attributed" categories. The latter can be attributed to a leader, an organisation, or the broader environment. Blaming leadership is evident when the leader associates the blame to oneself as an "internal locus of control" and prioritises individual agency and control into their failure framing (Liu, 2010). Company blame can be attributed when poor organisational culture or bureaucracy is present, whereas environmental blame shifts towards an "external locus of control" that attributes uncontrollable forces to be at play (Liu, 2010). The analysis of #Sandpapergate will explore the "attributed" categories of blame.

Leaders and the impact of the media

The media in its various forms, whether that is the 'old' or the so-called 'new' media, is a very powerful source of data and information about leaders, leader performance, and effectiveness (Chen & Meindl, 1991; Fairclough, 1995). As described by Liu (2010), and as discussed in relation to high performance management in Chapter 8, the media shapes and moulds the way we understand leaders through focussing the narrative around competence, trust, and/or authenticity. Through this process we have what is variously described as leader image construction.

The rise of the new media over the past decade has amplified the pressure on leaders to perform and manage their image under new levels of scrutiny (Frawley, 2017). The new media, where users are connected to each other and their followers, has meant the spread of information is incredibly fast leading to issues of accuracy and quality (Lock & Karg, 2016). The spread of this fast and often unstoppable wave of information, particularly when it relates to negative stories or events, has been termed an 'online firestorm'. An online firestorm occurs when negative word of mouth about leaders, organisations, groups, and/or certain individuals is propagated through social media networks, such as Facebook and Twitter, within seconds, minutes, or hours to a broad critical mass of people (Pfeffer, Zorbach, & Carley, 2014). A critical feature of online firestorms is that the messages communicated are generally opinions, not fact, and thus more often rumour rather than researched and fact-checked news.

The opinion-forming dynamics of social media platforms are thus influenced by a variety of interrelated characteristics. These include the speed and volume of social media that generate a high turnover of information; binary choices that users adopt during their decision-making processes to select what information they do and do not pass on to their followers; network clusters that connect and group users that echo the same information from different directions within their social network, thus creating the impression that everybody is talking about the same topic and with a similar opinion, also known as the "echo chamber" (Sunstein, 2001); unrestrained information flow that echoes and amplifies certain opinions and information; lack of diversity and creation of filter bubbles (Pariser, 2011) that highlights how people tend to connect with similar people in terms of age, gender, and socio-economic status, resulting in the promotion of similar interests and opinions; cross-media dynamics that acknowledge the role of social media in informing traditional media outlets to track stories during their infancy; and network-triggered decision processes that explore how opinions are formed and adopted.

The rise of social media has therefore impacted how traditional news agencies report shifting to a combined approach utilising both old and new media to break stories. This often results in traditional media agencies floating or releasing breaking stories through social media platforms and their websites before they commence more detailed research such as interviews and related fact checking (Pfeffer et al., 2014). Twitter, for instance, has been the key platform in "testing" the validity of stories and is regarded as the "fastest" platform due to its message length limits (Pfeffer et al., 2014). This discussion highlights how quickly the spread of information, whether accurate or not, can impact leaders from high-profile organisations when they are faced with a crisis or critical incident.

#Sandpapergate – the anatomy of a leadership crisis

(Written with Tessa McLachlan, UTS Business School)

The media content analysis found three common themes pertaining to blame and the leadership failure that was #Sandpapergate. These three themes are image, game integrity, and cricket culture and governance. The following section starts by explaining how the players, including the leader of the team (i.e. the Captain, Steve Smith), actively constructed their image after the game and then how the media interpreted this leader image construction.

Leader image construction

In the post-match press conference, Cameron Bancroft and Captain Steve Smith addressed the media while Vice-Captain David Warner did not attend. Whilst addressing their actions, Bancroft and Smith appeared solemn, apologetic, somewhat dismissive, and unaware of the impact this incident would have on their playing futures. Smith commented, *"I think I have made it clear, we're regrettable and we'll move on from this and hopefully we'll learn something from it"* (Smith, 2018). Bancroft and Smith also seemed "oblivious to the consequences" (ABC, 2018). In facing the

Continued

media's questions, Captain Smith was quick to protect his teammate and the integrity of the game. When asked if Smith was aware of Bancroft's actions, Smith stated:

> Yep, the leadership team knew about it. We spoke about it at lunch and I'm not proud of what's happened. It's not within the spirit of the game... It's not on, it's certainly not on and it won't happen again. I can promise you that - under my leadership.
>
> (Smith, 2018)

When asked if he would be stepping down as Captain, Smith confidently replied:

> No, I won't be considering stepping down. I still think I'm the right person for the job. Obviously today was a big mistake on my behalf and on the leadership group's behalf as well but I take responsibility as the captain - I need to take control of the ship. This is certainly something that I'm not proud of and something that [I hope I can] learn from and come back strong from ... We'll move past this. It's a big error in judgement but we'll learn from it and move past it.
>
> (Smith, 2018)

These quotes illustrate the lack of significance the players anticipated in response to their actions. Similarly, Bancroft addressed the media and remained somewhat accountable for his actions; he stated the following:

> Unfortunately, I was in the wrong place at the wrong time and I want to be here because I'm accountable for my actions as well. Like the captain said, I'm not proud of what's happened and I've got to live with the consequences, live with the damage to my own reputation that comes with and do my best to move forward and play cricket.
>
> (Bancroft, 2018)

A reporter probed further, asking Bancroft if he felt coerced by the leadership group or senior players, hinting at poor team culture; "*there's a suggestion that younger members of the team are often asked to do this kind of thing*" (Bancroft, 2018). Bancroft stated:

> I don't feel in this particular case it was that way. I was in the vicinity of the area when the leadership group were discussing it and look, I'll be honest with you, I was obviously nervous about it. With thousands, hundreds of cameras around, [getting caught] is always the risk, isn't it?
>
> (Bancroft, 2018)

Based on this narrative it can be argued that neither Smith nor Bancroft attempted to pass the blame.

In response to the cheating and the post-game press conference, the media reported themes of *failed leadership* and *inexperienced leadership*.

Steven Smith

When reporting on Smith's involvement, the media made frequent reference to Australia's past adoration of Smith, with comments including, *"Smith has been called one of the best players in cricket. He's a national hero - or was until now"* (Chiu, 2018). Similarly, they stated that Smith was *"one of the most personable, least calculating … and one of the more genuinely decent people to skipper the Australian team in recent decades"* (Lalor, 2018).

Speculation and questioning of Smith's capacity as a leader was a common theme presented by the experienced cricket journalists and writers. Craddock (2018) accused him *"of guiltily sitting on his hands as captain and not intervening"*, whereas other media expressed that Smith was *"just a kid"* (Knox, 2018) and that his *"boyish exterior hides … well, a boyish interior"* (Haigh, 2018). This suggests that he was *too young* to be in a leadership position. An article by Lalor (2018) paints a picture of a young, innocent, and naive man:

> Here was a man with no pretensions. An enthusiast. In Port Elizabeth he'd been out with his drone (the fad that's keeping them occupied this tour) and he'd filmed a pod of dolphins swimming beyond the waves. It was spectacular footage and he couldn't wait to show it, standing in his towel in the foyer of the team hotel, as excited as a kid with a new toy. Which he was.

Only one article, published by an international paper, *The Washington Post*, identified Smith as the instigator of the scandal: *"Smith noticed the South Africans had struggled with reverse swing … so Smith and other senior players devised a plan"* (Chiu, 2018). Typically, the media implied that this behaviour was out of character for Smith: for instance, *"the greatest shame is that moment of treachery is so out of character with everything else about Steve Smith"* (Lalor, 2018).

Cameron Bancroft

A common thread stated in the media reports was that Bancroft was impressionable and lacking in experience. Gallagher (2018) called it, *"nothing short of a disgrace that the premeditated plan devised by the senior and experienced players would allow the most inexperienced player to execute the*

Continued

act". Similarly, Lalor (2018) from *The Australian* newspaper sympathised with Bancroft who "*knew nothing but the environment he walked into*", yet still held him accountable for his "*Nuremberg style, just following orders*" answerability.

David Warner

Suspicion and questionability of Warner's leadership role were often implied in media reports. Typically, reports commented on Warner's temper that had historically "*presented management challenges*" (Haigh, 2018). Knox (2018) was the only reporter to openly defend Warner, who had just led the Australian T20 team in New Zealand and was "*obviously strung-out from his travel and workload*". Knox (2018) chronologically explored events since late December 2017, suggesting that Warner was more dedicated in his leadership role compared to Smith, who was regularly rested. Knox (2018) therefore suggested that Warner had reason to be disgruntled with his subordinate role in the team as Vice-Captain to Smith. Further, Knox (2018) offered that Warner was in a compromised mental state after altercations with South African match officials and players where he was 'sledged' over an alleged relationship his wife had before they were married with New Zealand All Black rugby player Sonny Bill Williams.

Haigh (2018) accused coach Darren Lehmann of being a consistent enabler of Warner, divulging that Lehmann always resolved Warner's "*abrasive competitive surface off the pitch*". This was evident when Lehmann dismissed the confrontation Warner had with South African player Quinton de Kock prior to the #Sandpapergate test match: "*(Lehmann) When it (the sledge) crossed the line he (Warner) defended his family and women in general, so from my point of view I thought he did the right thing*" (Haigh, 2018).

Social media word of mouth

The controversial incident 'exploded' across social media. In waking to the events unfolding in Cape Town, large numbers took to Twitter to voice their dismay and outrage. This included the most recently retired Australian Cricket Captain, Michael Clark, who tweeted, "*WHAT THE ... HAVE I JUST WOKEN UP TO. Please tell me this is a bad dream*". Former Australian cricket great Shane Warne tweeted,

> Very disappointed with the pictures I saw on our coverage here in Cape Town. If proven, the alleged ball tampering is what we all think it is - then I hope Steve Smith and Darren Lehmann do the press conference to clean this mess up!

Subsequently, the Clark tweet received 3,852 "retweets" and 17,524 "likes", while the Warne tweet received 1,709 "retweets" and 9,783 "likes", demonstrating the intense speed and large volume of the social media word of mouth.

Chui (2018) shed light on the mockery of the situation that saw Air New Zealand post a Facebook video calling Bancroft a "*naughty boy*" and suggested he visit for a holiday to "*escape the heat back home*". Chui (2018) further commented on fans' tirade of comedic memes (pictures) and GIFs (short videos). Moreover, moral outrage was seen on social media platforms that targeted the players' partners. Comments made on Bancroft's 21-year-old partner's Instagram account were highlighted in a news article titled "*WAGs Caught up in Ball Tampering Scandal*" (2018) and included "*f**king filthy human*" and "*YOUR BOY HAS DISGRACED YOUR COUNTRY. CHEATER!*"

Game integrity

Defending the game's *integrity* was evident in the media's attempt to shed light on cheating throughout the global cricket community and sport in general. However, speculation of the Australian team's success to date and how this incident would impact Australia's sporting pride were also common sub-themes.

History of ball tampering: "everyone does it" mindset

Numerous media reports made reference to the long history of ball tampering in the sport with comments such as "*South Africans know a bit about ball tampering, having been accused and convicted of it in the past*" (Knox, 2018); "*Ball tampering is practised by virtually every team in some way shape or form … this is not an extraordinary offence*" (ABC, 2018); and "*when it comes to sports, cheating isn't all that unusual*" (Chiu, 2018). Cricket analyst Simon Hughes offered that despite this history of cheating in cricket, the integrity of the sport has always prevailed: "*there's always been skulduggery in cricket but it's always had this status as a sport where people behave well and respect each other*" (Chiu, 2018). This suggests that such tactics are regarded as just part of the game and therefore an attempt to downgrade the severity of the incident and reduce culpability.

Another aspect reported in the media referred to the integrity and validity of the Australian team's success over past cricket seasons. During the press conference, Smith was asked if this was the first time such cheating had taken place under his leadership: "*You can ask questions as much as you like but I can promise you that this is the first time it has happened*" (Smith, 2018). However, given that a similar reverse swing had been seen at the

Continued

previous match the reporter warned, *"now obviously, when things like this happen, there will be question marks"* (Smith, 2018). Similarly, Knox (2018) speculated on the success of the team during the 2017–2018 Ashes series, when *"England questioned the sugar Bancroft kept in his pocket. The officials accepted his explanation that he preferred sugar, over the binge supply of sugar drinks and snacks that go to players on the field, for his energy"* (Knox, 2018).

Sensationalised and nationalistic language was adopted throughout various media reports. Chiu (2018) played to the patriotism of Australian cricket: *"the incident has embroiled the cricket-loving country in scandal and broken the hearts of die-hard fans"*, quoting the country's Prime Minister, who offered that wearing the *"baggy green"* cap holds higher national esteem than any political role. In an ABC (2018) radio interview, Gideon Haigh, the senior cricket writer with *The Australian* newspaper, considered the future implications of the scandal: *"I don't think I have ever seen the Australian public as united in their disapproval of an Australian team"*, believing the footage would act as *"a symbol of how far Australia is willing to go for an advantage for future generations"*.

Cricket culture and governance

Poor team culture was a prominent theme that emerged from the media reports, but this was contrasted with the discussion on the role of mateship. Extensive speculation of the role or lack thereof played by the national governing body Cricket Australia was also revealed. Knox (2018), for instance, attributed the team's arrogance to be the key ingredient in the poor morale, which saw them act as *"classic bullies, considerably keener on dishing out than taking"*. Similarly, Stensholt (2018) questioned how the *"complicit management team"* had been allowed to create a culture *"where cheating is considered a way to winning"*.

The media also speculated how the ego of Smith and Warner may have impacted and influenced their poor judgement. Haigh (2018) believed that both Smith and Warner had developed *"man-eating grievances"* – as alluded to earlier, Warner, due to the vilification of his wife, and Smith, due to his on-field *"nemesis"*, South African fast bowler Kagiso Rabada, escaping suspension for unsportsmanlike offences. Knox (2018) blamed the Australian team's "sense of victimhood", which can be used to *"unify teams"* and create an *"institutionalised and inward-looking, win-at-all-costs moral code, and an anger towards the outside world"*. (This point also relates to the discussion on social identity and leadership in Chapter 2, in that the strengthening of the in-group impacts the response to the out-group).

The notion of mateship was used by some in the media as an explanation of Smith's poor decision-making. Smith commented during the post-match press conference that a lunchtime discussion took place *"between the leadership group"* when the decision was made to tamper with the ball (Smith, 2018). When pressured further Smith stated, *"It was the leadership group. I'm not naming names, but the leadership group were talking about it and Bangers [Bancroft] was there at the time and we spoke about it"* (Smith, 2018). Smith maintained accountability for the team's actions whilst also spreading culpability. Craddock (2018) stated, *"the consensus is that Smith was covering for Warner"*. This point was supported by a tweet posted by New South Wales and former Australian test player, Moises Henriques, who theorised that Smith used the collective language to *"take the heat off a young Cameron Bancroft, not realising the outrage that would follow"*.

As stated by cricket journalist Peter Lalor (2018) Smith *"saw a bus headed for Bancroft, knew that it wasn't right and attempted to throw himself in front of it"* and challenged his audience to consider who else in the team would have tried to *"share the pain"* as he did. Conversely, the media were quick to target Warner and his role and influence in the poor decision-making, especially when there was no formal comment made by theVice-Captain immediately after the incident was discovered. Craddock (2018) argued, *"there is a feeling among other players that the opener (David Warner) was willing to throw everyone else under the bus in a bid to take the heat off his own role in the controversy"*.

Blaming Cricket Australia

The media frequently commented on the role of Cricket Australia in how the national team's culture manifested. Stensholt (2018) addressed the *"How we play"* section in the organisation's most recent five-year plan that proclaimed *"make every ball ... be relentless ... play to win"*. Haigh (2018) also touched on the irony of how Cricket Australia quietly dropped the *"spirit of cricket"* phrase from its published strategy in replacement of *"jaded slogans"*. Knox (2018) offered, *"this disgrace didn't happen during one night, the cycle of hubris was long in the making"*, thus looking beyond the blame of the three players.

Stensholt (2018) also revealed that the Australian Cricketers Association Annual Report called on Cricket Australia to review its *"behaviours and tactics"*. This to some degree illustrates the awareness yet complacency and inability to deal with a poor organisational culture. An article by Haigh (2018) exposed the toxicity of Cricket Australia's culture during a so-called 'independent review' of the national male teams seven years ago, in which players were shocked to find the Cricket Australia CEO, James Sutherland, present when they were interviewed.

Haigh (2018) accused Cricket Australia of caring *"little about the sports image, except as a brand or product"*, drawing from comments made by the

Continued

senior commercial executive of the organisation, Ben Amarfio, five years ago when he said, "*controversy in sport was not a problem — it could even be advantageous*" and that it could create "*a lot more interest in your brand and your sport*".

From a similar position, the former coach of the Australian team Mickey Arthur, now coach of Pakistan, blamed Cricket Australia for "*demonstrating no real willingness or desire to improve the culture within their organisation from season to season. That could lead to only one conclusion. An explosion*" (Haigh, 2018). Similarly, Gallagher (2018) accused Cricket Australia of "*lacking independence and accountability*", blaming these issues to be a result of "*poor governance and poor culture*".

Interestingly, Gallagher (2018) argued that the CEO, James Sutherland, had been there way too long, commenting that his 17-year tenure as CEO is "*out of step*" with modern management practices and succession planning. Haigh (2018) further commented on Sutherland's unusual tenure as CEO and described the man as "*a tall, grave and rather shy figure who wears a jacket and tie like a suit of armour*".

In a statement released by Cricket Australia (2018), Sutherland placed emphasis on the negative impact the ball tampering incident would have on the game: "*I understand the appetite for urgency given the reputation of Australia as a sporting nation has been damaged in the eyes of many*"; he also admitted that the "*issue goes beyond the technical nature of the offences*". At the same press conference, Sutherland revealed that he had not spoken to Steve Smith due to the time difference with South Africa (Bradford, 2018). Sutherland's poor effort at the press conference resulted in a tidal wave of negative word of mouth via social media unfold with some tweets calling him "spineless" and a "failed leader".

A week after the event the narrative in the media started to shift with the three players arriving home from South Africa. During this period, three themes emerged from the media and included *sympathy, mental health*, and *supportive social media word of mouth*. In addition, another two themes started to be revealed pertaining to blame, that being the *role of the coach* and *Australia's (unrealistic sporting) expectations*. When the players arrived back from South Africa each conducted separate press conferences, which were attended by rarely seen large numbers of both sport and non-sport media, and were shown live across free-to-air and subscription television and commercial and public radio.

Outrage to sympathy

When addressing the media in Sydney after arriving back in Australia, Smith "*sobbed uncontrollably as he detailed his regret … He went on manfully, ashamed of his actions but not ashamed to show the world how abject he feels*" (Lalor, 2018). Smith's vulnerability resonated with many in the media, and what they viewed a week earlier as outrage now had shifted to support: "*No politician would ever submit themselves to such raw examination or regret. Captains have cried publicly before but there was something about this*" (Lalor, 2018). Again, Smith refused to implicate others: "*I want to make clear, as captain of the Australian cricket team, I take full responsibility*" (ABC News, 2018a).

Bancroft also addressed the media upon arriving back in Perth, stating that "*it is something I will regret for the rest of my life*" (Daily Telegraph, 2018). This saw a shift in media headlines to supportive perspectives such as "*Cricket world throws support behind Steve Smith, Cameron Bancroft*" (Daily Telegraph, 2018). In comparison, the media were generally critical of Warner's approach to his apology, which was initially delivered through a post on Twitter where he stated, "*mistakes have been made which have damaged cricket*" (Davutovic, 2018). Upon questioning by the media when he arrived back at Sydney Airport, Warner said, "*At the moment, my priority is to get these kids in bed and rest up and let my mind be clear so I can think and talk to you in a couple of days*" (Daily Telegraph, 2018).

State of mind

Particularly in response to Smith's emotional press conference, the media began to look at the broader repercussions that the ball tampering incident was having, not only on his career but also on his state of mind. Headlines reflecting this sentiment included "*Steve Smith is a broken man, and still one to be proud of*" (Lalor, 2018) and statements such as "*He (Smith) lives for cricket, which is just as well because the system offers him nothing else, except money*" (Haigh, 2018) and "*people are concerned for him … He cuts such a lonely, devastated figure in the corridors of the hotel*" (Lalor, 2018).

The coach

As time progressed, greater accountability and blame was redirected to the coach, Darren Lehmann. A common view expressed was that Lehmann may have encouraged the questionable behaviour and resulting culture: "*the coach sets the agenda … He's not exactly the retiring type*" (Lalor, 2018). This perspective was compounded by previous comments made by Lehmann on ball tampering in test cricket: "*Obviously there's techniques used by both sides to get the ball reversing. That's just the way the game goes. I have no problem with it. Simple*" (Haigh, 2018).

Not long though after the three players held their emotional press conferences Lehmann decided to announce his resignation. According to

Continued

Davutovic (2018), his resignation was prompted by the teary press conferences of Smith and Bancroft. Lehmann stated, *"I'm ultimately responsible for the culture of the team"*. Davutovic (2018) further pointed out that Lehmann's *"family had received a torrent of abuse and that he had not slept since Sandpapergate broke on Saturday"*.

Haigh (2018) however wrote that Lehmann resigned *"before he was pushed [by CA]"*. This view was supported by the points made at James Sutherland's media address where he stated that *"Discipline, consistency of behaviour and accountability for performance are all key ingredients that need to improve. And we see that the head coach is ultimately responsible for that"*. In other words, the senior coach needs to take a fair portion of the blame for what occurred in South Africa.

National expectations

In writing about #Sandpapergate cricket writer Gideon Haigh suggested that the Australian people and their *"intense connection"* to cricket resulted in high and unrealistic expectations of their cricketers in wanting them to *"embody special values"* and *"national traits"*. In a similar vein, Lalor (2018) stated that Australians *"cherish cricket"* and hold the national team to such a high standard *"because it is sport that gives us so much pride and hope"*. Lalor (2018) believed Australians *"want more from cricketers than from elected leaders or our holy men"* and challenged his readers to consider the repercussion for Australian politicians that *"lie and cheat and stay in office unscathed"*. This view suggests that Australia, as a sporting nation, is partly to blame for the failed leadership of the national cricket team.

Discussion

In applying Liu's (2010) failed leadership framework it is useful to explore how blame was initially framed and dispersed and how it shifted over time. As proposed by Liu (2010) in explaining the how and why failure occurred three levels can be analysed: leader, company, or environment. (This perspective also has similarities to the ideas discussed in Chapter 8 on high performance management and the multiple levels of analysis required when exploring leadership success and failure).

In the initial stage of #Sandpapergate the blame for leadership failure was projected clearly on those closest to the incident: in this case Smith as Captain, Warner as Vice-Captain, and Lehmann as Coach. Smith, in particular, along with Bancroft, admitted his errors early, therefore associating blame with himself and demonstrating individual agency as an "internal locus of control" (Liu, 2010). Smith demonstrated accountability straightaway with the statement "*I made a serious error of judgment and I now understand the consequences. It was a failure of leadership, of my leadership*" (Smith, 2018). In hindsight, Warner was too slow to react, with his first statement to the media taking place days after the incident and delivered via a Twitter post: "*Mistakes have been made which have damaged cricket. I apologise for my part and take responsibility for it*" (Bailey, 2018). This delay and the avoidance of the press, and thus choice of media channel, illustrated *poor leadership image construction* and *impression management* that was most likely attributed to Warner's unfavourable media portrayal throughout the initial reports. This included media statements that Warner was the "*central character in Australian cricket's ball-tampering crisis*" (Barrett, 2018b) describing him as the "*chief conspirator*" (Margan, 2018).

It is important to note that Bancroft, although not in an official leadership position but as a member of the national team, did not fully account blame to himself, showing more concern for his future career: "*I'm not proud of what's happened and I've got to live with the consequences, live with the damage to my own reputation*" (Bancroft, 2018). Bancroft also offered *environmental factors* to blame when remarking, "*unfortunately, I was in the wrong place at the wrong time*" (Bancroft, 2018). However, given the infancy of his career and lack of experience in the test cricket arena, it would seem that this protected his role and character from greater media scrutiny.

By addressing their wrongdoings through the media, Smith and Bancroft demonstrated *authentic leadership* that can be considered as the ethically correct way to respond (Liu, 2010). Moreover, by addressing the public through the media, both players displayed effective *impression management* by admitting their failures, demonstrating genuine repentance and desire to rectify their mistakes (Kusy & Essex, 2007; Tucker et al., 2006). This was particularly evident after the players delivered separate press conferences upon arriving back in Australia, which saw a softening of the placing of blame and media sentiments displaying more a sympathetic attitude: "*Smith and Bancroft have been praised by fans for their heartfelt public apologies over the ball tampering saga after addressing the media in emotional press conferences*" (Crawley, 2018). This complements the notion of Shamir et al. (2005) that when leaders recount previous failures and demonstrate perseverance, it earns "*both self respect and respect from others*".

Given Smith's status prior to the incident as the "golden boy" of Australian cricket, it could be argued that this influenced how the media continued to shape his leader image. As Fairclough (1995) offered, the media holds the power to recontextualise and distort a leader's message, either favourably or to a leader's detriment. This would offer an explanation

Continued

as to why the media attributed Smith's *environment* to his failure, such as Lalor's (2018) report that stated *poor culture* was prevalent before his captaincy: "*the ceiling was sagging in the dressing room long before he entered it. The roof had been leaking for years. Nobody was interested in the rising damp because there was so much sunshine.*"

Similarly, sentiments of support filtered across social media word of mouth, complementing Liu's (2010) finding that leaders possess the power to control what their followers consume via *image building*, that is, "*actively articulating and expressing their self-image to bolster their image of competence*". (Also see the relevant example of Team Sky Cycling and the leadership of David Brailsford in Chapter 8). This shift was displayed across social media, evident in supportive tweets, including Australian politician Bill Shorten's offering, "*good people make mistakes*"; comedian Andy Lee's stating it was the "*best way to start the road to redemption*"; and British commentator Piers Morgan's declaring it's "*time to call off the dogs*". This supports Goffee and Jones's (2001) thesis that admitting mistakes and revealing weaknesses can improve a leader's accessibility and even result in solidarity amongst their followers. Moreover, the *speed and volume* of such social media word of mouth should be acknowledged, exemplified by Piers Morgan's tweet alone that received 16,500 "likes" almost immediately.

Contrastingly, Warner demonstrated *poor authentic leadership* and *impression management*. This was evident in his lack of presence and avoidance of the press in general. It could be argued that such avoidance made Warner vulnerable to negative framing of blame. Craddock (2018) particularly demonstrated this with highly speculative language, offering Warner's absence as "*a sign he has gone rogue*". Interestingly, Warner's blame was often explained by *environmental factors* that attributed to a bad frame of mind, such as the off-field confrontation with South Africa's Quinton de Kock, the vilification of his wife, and his T20 efforts prior to the test series.

Warner's framing of blame was particularly highlighted after Smith and Bancroft's individual press conferences, which saw social media word of mouth draw parallels between the approaches to leadership. Former England Captain Michael Vaughan tweeted, "*2 out of the 3 players fronting up to the media… Speaking honestly and in great regret… 1 speaking through a statement on social media..!!!.*" Similarly, this saw negative word of mouth propagate, evident in posts made on the online article "*A Stain on the Game*" (Noyes, 2018), which included "*Hopefully he's sincere. It would be sad to think his apology was all about his bank-balance*" and "*Since when has writing something via Twitter constituted spoken word? Warner hasn't broken his silence on anything. Anyone could've written that on Twitter on his behalf.*" This public reaction can be explained by Kusy and Essex (2007) in that, "insincere apologies can reflect negatively on the leader as weak, incompetent and deceitful".

An interesting development over time was the redirection of blame towards the Coach, Lehmann. As revealed, his resignation was instigated by Smith and Bancroft's individual press conferences which saw Lehmann consider account for his role within the scandal: *"After seeing events in the media today with Steve Smith and Cameron Bancroft, the feeling is that Australian cricket needs to move forward, and this is the right thing to do"* (Lehmann, 2018). Lehmann did so via his own press conference, in which he attributed the blame to his leadership:

> I'm ultimately responsible for the culture of the team and I've been thinking about my position for a while, despite telling the media yesterday that I'm not resigning, after viewing Steve and Cameron's hurting, it's only fair that I make this decision.
>
> (Lehmann, 2018)

Like Smith and Bancroft, Lehmann illustrated best practice in terms of *authentic leadership* and *impression management*. Interestingly, Cricket Australia attributed blame directly to Lehmann, declaring him as *"ultimately responsible"*. This direct attribution of blame was the only finding that did not offer one's own involvement as the "internal locus of control" to explain *how the failure occurred*, thus confirming media sentiments of Cricket Australia's problematic organisational culture.

Much blame, as demonstrated in the aforementioned findings, was attributed to Cricket Australia. As Liu (2010) offered, *company blame* can be attributed when *poor organisational culture* is present. Cricket Australia's poor management of cricketing culture was clear throughout media reports in attributing and shaping blame, including Cricket Australia's revised strategic plan, which removed phrases like the *"spirit of cricket"* for more aggressive language (Haigh, 2018); statements made by the commercial executive that scandals can be "advantageous" to obtaining publicity and brand awareness (Haigh, 2018); prior recommendations by industry associations for Cricket Australia to review its *"behavior and tactics"* (Stensholt, 2018); the exposure of Cricket Australia's *"independent review"*, which took place with the CEO James Sutherland sitting in when players were interviewed (Haigh, 2018); and comments from former national Coaches that had previously blamed Cricket Australia for *"demonstrating no real willingness or desire to improve the culture within their organisation"* (Haigh, 2018).

Critically, the failure of a leader is of great consequence as it ultimately reflects on the performance of the organisation and the individuals

Continued

themselves (Liu, 2010). With this in mind, it does raise questions as to why Cricket Australia allowed Smith and Bancroft to hold a post-match conference with the footage already confirmed. As the *"custodians of the game"* (Gallagher, 2018), one would question Cricket Australia's efforts in protecting the image and integrity of the game. As many have suggested, from a media standpoint, the integrity of sport is rarely commented on unless it appears to be absent (Schulenkorf & Frawley, 2017). This does open Cricket Australia's up to criticism for the lack of an initial directive, not only to protect the *integrity of the sport* but also to protect that of the players.

Finally, the media influenced and shaped the framing of blame through highly speculative and non-committal language to manipulate blame in the reader's mind most likely with the benefit of leaks from inside Cricket Australia. This included statements such as, *"It's anticipated Smith and Warner will be stripped of their leadership duties and receive long bans, while coach Darren Lehmann is also in line to be sacked"* (Craddock, 2018), and phrases like *"it's anticipated that"* and *"it is understood that"*. Similarly, Gallagher (2018) stated that the incident had *"led to a significant national reaction, perhaps unparalleled in the modern era"*. In doing so, such sensationalised language suggested to readers that the nature of the text was the *general consensus*. This sees two key elements of the opinion-forming dynamics of Pfeffer et al. (2014) come into play: *speed and volume* of word of mouth, and *cross-media dynamics*, in that social media informed traditional media to track stories during their infancy. Moreover, the use of Twitter from prominent figures, including Warner, solidified the notion of Pfeffer et al. (2014) that *"Twitter seems to play a critical role in the propagation of online firestorms"*.

Conclusion

This analysis demonstrates the impact the media has on shaping and dispersing blame about sport scandals, in this case specifically #Sandpapergate. Through the application of Liu's (2010) failed leadership framework it was shown that the media influenced the framing of blame across the three attributed factors: leaders, company, and environment. This study confirms that leadership failure is best managed *proactively* and *authentically*. Furthermore, rectification should be pursued through traditional media channels to limit the media's capacity to misinterpret and manipulate a leader's message. Failure to do this can result in the "floating" of rumours as fact on social media platforms, which then can result in the propagation of *online firestorms* and associated negative word of mouth. As outlined by Liu (2010) it can be a "Herculean task" for leaders to restore their image in the public eye, because they tend to view "mistakes and failures weighed against not only their leadership capabilities, but character and moral integrity".

Case study – failed leadership: Swimming Australia and London 2012

By Lloyd Rothwell, UTS Business School

"The cornerstone of any well-functioning organisation is good leadership" (Independent Review Panel, 2013).

The Australian Swimming Team departed for the London 2012 Olympic Games with high hopes. After all, they boasted one of the world's most exciting rising stars, James Magnussen, who was the reigning world champion is his main event: the 100 m freestyle. At the Australian Olympic Trials in Adelaide, Magnussen put his rivals on notice, easily winning in a blistering time, and then proclaimed "brace yourself", displaying a swagger not often seen in swimming. While the mainstream media was excited about the possibility of a "gold rush", swimming experts were more circumspect. No one, though, would go on to predict the sharp decline in performance from Beijing 2008, when Australia's swimmers won 20 Olympic medals, including six gold medals, compared with London 2012, when the Women's 100 m freestyle relay recorded the only gold medal in a total of ten medals overall. In the aftermath it emerged that there were serious organisational concerns amongst members of the team, including allegations of poor behaviour, bullying, harassment, misuse of prescription medication, and a fractured relationship between some athletes.

These incidents, however, did not occur in isolation. The dysfunctional nature of the team was highlighted in two reports conducted after the Games; the first by respected consultant Dr Pippa Grange and the second by an independent panel jointly commissioned by Swimming Australia and the Australian Sports Commission. Both reports found a failure in leadership across multiple levels. In hindsight, a number of warning signs were exhibited in the lead up to London 2012 that should have been addressed by the relevant leaders.

1   Key staff movements

There was significant organisational change at Swimming Australia after the Beijing Games. The long-term CEO Glenn Tasker, who had substantial experience within the sport of swimming, resigned in the months prior to the Games to leave the head office based in Canberra and return to his native Sydney. The new CEO was recruited after previously being appointed to the Board of Directors several months earlier; however that was the extent of his swimming experience. That notwithstanding, the newly appointed boss did have a wealth of experience within a highly commercial sport, and this reportedly played a key role in his appointment. Then, in 2010, during a restructuring of the high performance division within Swimming Australia, the Head Coach departed after six years in the role.

Continued

2   Individualised preparation

The high performance approach adopted to prepare for London 2012 was formulated to decentralise athlete preparations. This was seen as a more flexible philosophy as opposed to previous rigid structures and allowed swimmers to mostly prepare in their "home programs" rather than coming together in camps. However, an unintended consequence of this decision, that was later acknowledged, was that this decentralisation made it very difficult for the team to build a cohesive culture when they were apart. One swimmer noted the decline of team spirit over several years and attributed this to poor leadership within the organisation. One journalist reported, "The swimmer said this had created 'general unrest' within the group and the team culture had been eroded as individual swimmers pursued their own interests, undermining the overall performance of the team" (Jeffrey, 2012).

3   Team selection / Lack of experience

A total of 24 out of 47 swimmers made their Olympic debut at London 2012. As Coaches are selected based on the performance of their swimmers, the lack of experience also included members of the Coaching staff. Inexplicitly, there was not a sport psychologist selected for London 2012 as part of the support team. These would prove key factors when the squad was forced to deal with adversity after a poor start to the Olympics. Later reviews indicated that team culture was left to develop of its own accord rather than drawing on those amongst the team that did have significant Olympic experience. Speaking after the Games, former elite swimmer and Olympic medallist Geoff Huegill was keen to press the importance of leadership from the Coaching team:

> I think the biggest thing to look at is the coaches, because the coaches have to take responsibility for this. If the coaches don't take responsibility for these athletes and for the leadership that needs to be shown, then they're ultimately just as much to blame as the athletes.
>
> (ABC, 2013)

These factors show the need for clear, strong, inclusive leadership. Instead, once the team got off to a poor start at the Games, problems and divisions were magnified. As a result, once the negativity began to fester, it became increasingly difficult to rectify. On the reports of bullying, breaststroker and long-time national team member Leisel Jones was one person who did speak up. She later told the *Courier Mail* newspaper:

> If something is against my values I'm pretty vocal against that and people are pretty clear on how I feel. Definitely if I see something that

is not quite right I'm very, very happy to stand up and speak up about it. It's against my values and I'm pretty strong against that.

(Balym, 2012)

Following the Games two independent reviews were conducted, with the culture of the team labelled as "toxic". In the aftermath the President, CEO, and Head Coach of Swimming Australia all resigned from their positions.

Given what transpired, it's arguable that Swimming Australia didn't have adequate strategies in place around leadership development and succession planning. All levels of leadership across the sport were criticised, with a specific focus on the Board, senior management, and high performance functional area. The failure of effective leadership raises numerous issues, including effective governance, strategy, marketing, organisational and high performance structures, accountability of key personnel, recruitment and selection, leadership development, organisational culture, and the impact these functions have on the culture and performance of a team of elite sportspeople.

The independent panel described the importance of governance and administration in delivering a successful high performance programme, noting, "this outcome is the final link of a chain which begins with the Board and executive management as a result of strategic decisions that impact the sport" (Independent Review Panel, 2013). The "Bluestone Review" strongly recommended the introduction of leadership development programmes for athletes and Coaches and highlighted a "dire need to develop and enable leadership throughout swimming, and to orient people to consider leadership as personal, not just functional" (Grange, 2013).

References

ABC News (2018a). "'I don't think I've ever seen an Australian public as united in their disapproval of an Australian team' Cricket Writer Gideon Haigh", *ABC News*, 26 March 2018, viewed 20 April 2018, http://www.abc.net.au/news/2018-03-25/gideon-haigh-calls-australian-cricket-team-sneaky-and-reckless/9584962

ABC News (2018b). "Steve Smith apologises for ball-tampering incident after arriving back in Australia", *ABC News*, 29 March 2018, viewed 1 June 2018, http://www.abc.net.au/news/2018-03-29/steve-smith-apologises-for-ball-tampering-scandal/9603670

Australian Broadcasting Corporation (2013). "Review slams toxic culture in Olympic swim team", *ABC News* Online, 20 February.

Bailey, S. (2018). "Australian cricketer David Warner apologises: 'Mistakes have been made'", *The West Australian*, 29 March 2018, viewed 1 June 2018, https://thewest.com.au/sport/cricket/australian-cricketer-david-warner-apologises-mistakes-have-been-made-ng-b88790488z

Balym, T. (2012). "Leisel Jones confirms she confronted swimmers who were bullying teammate at Olympic Games", *The Courier Mail*, 18 November.

Bancroft, C. (2018). "Transcript: The Smith and Bancroft ball-tampering confession", *Sydney Morning Herald*, 25 March 2018, viewed 20 April 2018, https://www.smh.com.au/sport/cricket/transcript-the-smith-and-bancroft-ball-tampering-confession-20180325-p4z65c.html

Barrett, C. (2018a). "Dark day for Australian cricket as Steve Smith admits plan to cheat", *Sydney Morning Herald*, 25 March 2018, viewed 10 May 2018, https://www.smh.com.au/sport/cricket/dark-day-for-australian-cricket-as-steve-smith-admits-plan-to-cheat-20180325-p4z63q.html

Barrett, C. (2018b). "David Warner at heart of ball-tampering scandal", *Sydney Morning Herald*, 26 March 2018, viewed 10 June 2018, https://www.smh.com.au/sport/cricket/david-warner-at-heart-of-ball-tampering-scandal-20180326-p4z6d3.html

Bradford, B. (2018). "Cricket Australia boss James Sutherland slammed for 'spineless' press conference following ball-tampering revelations", *Sporting News*, 24 March 2018, viewed 16 April 2018, http://www.sportingnews.com/au/cricket/news/cricket-australia-boss-james-sutherland-slammed-for-spineless-press-conferencefollowing-ball-tampering-revelations/g0cjju0yedyp13okp1f88dktb

Chen, C., & Meindl, J. (1991). The construction of leadership images in the popular press: The case of Donald Burr and people express. *Administrative Science Quarterly, 36*, 521–551.

Chiu, A. (2018). "'Sandpapergate' cheating scandal rocks Australian cricket: 'It beggars belief,' says prime minister", *The Washington Post*, 29 March 2018, viewed 20 April 2018, https://www.washingtonpost.com/news/morning-mix/wp/2018/03/28/sandpapergate-cheating-scandal-rocks-australian-cricket-it-beggars-belief-says-prime-minister/?noredirect=on&utm_term=.5473870deea0

Craddock, R. (2018). "'Rogue' Warner sparks feud with fast bowlers", *The Australian*, 27 March 2018, viewed 20 May 2018, https://www.theaustralian.com.au/sport/cricket/rogue-warner-sparks-feud-with-fast-bowlers/news-story/0b06607446400a294cb41fcacc12e61f

Crawley, P. (2018). "Fans defend Australian cricketers after statements following ball tampering saga", *Daily Telegraph*, 30 March 2018, viewed 10 June 2018, https://www.dailytelegraph.com.au/sport/cricket/fans-defend-australian-cricketers-after-statements-following-ball-tampering-saga/news-story/8946b6146c6ace04b7609a827442eff3

Cricket Australia (2018). *Cricket Australia Statement*, 28 March 2018, viewed 10 May 2018, https://www.cricketaustralia.com.au/media/media-releases/cricket-australia-statement/2018-03-28

Daily Telegraph (2018). "Cricket world throws support behind Steve Smith, Cameron Bancroft", *Daily Telegraph*, 30 March 2018, viewed 1 June 2018, https://www.dailytelegraph.com.au/sport/cricket/cricket-world-throws-support-behind-steve-smith-cameron-bancroft/news-story/f919cbd4c99a36064b46fca730639063

Davutovic, D. (2018). "Darren Lehmann quits as Australian cricket coach", *The Australian*, 30 March 2018, viewed 1 June 2018, https://www.theaustralian.com.au/sport/cricket/darren-lehmann-quits-as-australian-cricket-coach/news-story/2723612c39982acd2073222d53d51f41

Eagly, A. (2005). Achieving relational authenticity in leadership: Does gender matter? *Leadership Quarterly, 16*, 459–474.

Fairclough, N. (1995). *Critical discourse analysis: A critical study of language.* New York: Longman.

Fairhurst, G. (2007). *Discursive leadership: In conversation with leadership psychology.* Thousand Oaks, CA: Sage Publications.

Frawley, S. (2017). *Managing sport mega-events.* London: Routledge.

Frawley, S., Favaloro, D., & Schulenkorf, N. (2018). Experience-based leadership development and professional sport organizations. *Journal of Sport Management, 32*(2), 123–134.

Gallagher, D. (2018). "Cricket Australia clearly has a corporate culture problem", *Australian Financial Review*, 26 March 2018, viewed 10 May 2018, https://www.afr.com/opinion/columnists/cricket-australia-clearly-has-a-corporate-culture-problem-20180326-h0xza2

Grange, P. (2013). *A review of culture and leadership in Australian Olympic Swimming.* Sydney: Bluestone Edge.

Goffee, R., & Jones, G. (2001). Why should anyone be led by you? *Harvard Business Review, 78*(55), 62–70.

Grint, K. (2001). *The arts of leadership.* New York: Oxford University Press.

Haigh, G. (2018). "CA finally gets one over Warner", *The Australian*, 31 March 2018, viewed 10 May 2018, https://www.theaustralian.com.au/news/inquirer/steve-smith-david-warner-sent-home-but-who-will-judge-the-cricket-australia-suits/news-story/4b1dcce97ba702a6fef06f99c4eafe15?login=1

Independent Review Panel. (2013). *Independent review of swimming.* Canberra: Australian Sports Commission.

Jeffrey, N. (2012). "Disciplinary issues undercut the morale and unity of the Australian swimming team at London Games", *The Australian Newspaper*, 12 September.

Katz, N. (2001). Sports teams as a model for workplace teams: Lessons and liabilities. *Academy of Management Executive, 15*(3), 56–67.

Kellerman, B. (2006). When should a leader apologize—and when not? *Harvard Business Review, 84*(4), 72–81.

Knox, M. (2018). "For Australian cricket, arrogance rewarded just led to more arrogance", *Sydney Morning Herald*, 26 March 2018, viewed 15 April 2018, https://www.smh.com.au/sport/cricket/for-australian-cricket-arrogance-rewarded-just-led-to-more-arrogance-20180326-p4z6c5.html

Kusy, M., & Essex, L. (2007). Recovering from leadership mistakes. *Leader to Leader, 44*, 14–19.

Lalor, P. (2018). "The tragedy of Steve Smith's fall from grace", *The Australian*, 28 March 2018, viewed 15 May 2018, https://www.theaustralian.com.au/sport/opinion/peter-lalor/the-tragedy-of-steve-smiths-fall-from-grace/news-story/1751adf4500ef142a960ada4ede7297c

Lasswell, H. D. (1948). The structure and function of communication in society. *The Communication of Ideas, 37*, 215–228.

Lehmann, D. (2018). "Lehmann's emotional resignation speech", *SBS News*, 30 March 2018, viewed 10 June 2018, https://www.sbs.com.au/news/lehmann-s-emotional-resignation-speech

Liu, H. (2010). When leaders fail: A typology of failures and framing strategies. *Management Communication Quarterly, 24*(2), 232–259.

Lock, D., & Karg, A. (2016). New media development and strategies for sport mega-events: the Olympic Games and the Football World Cup. In S. Frawley (Ed.), *Managing sport mega-events* (pp. 135–152). London: Routledge.

Macnamara, J. (2005). Media content analysis: Its uses, benefits and best practice methodology. *Asia Pacific Public Relations Journal, 6*(1), 1–34.

Margan, M. (2018). "Cricket scandal David Warner named chief conspirator", *Daily Mail*, 27 March 2018, viewed 1 June 2018, http://www.dailymail.co.uk/news/article-5546823/Cricket-scandal-David-Warner-named-chief-conspirator.html

Neundorf, K. (2002). *The content analysis guidebook*. New York, Thousands Oaks: Sage.

Noyes, J. (2018). "'A stain on the game': Warner apologises for ball-tampering scandal", *Sydney Morning Herald*, 29 March 2018, viewed 10 June 2018, https://www.smh.com.au/sport/a-stain-on-the-game-warner-apologises-for-ball-tampering-scandal-20180329-p4z6yd.html

Pariser, E. (2011). *The filter bubble: What the internet is hiding from you*. New York: Penguin Press.

Peachey, J. W., Zhou, Y., Damon, Z. J., & Burton, L. J. (2015). Forty years of leadership research in sport management: A review, synthesis, and conceptual framework. *Journal of Sport Management, 29*(5), 570–587.

Pfeffer, J., Zorbach, T., & Carley, K. (2014). Understanding online firestorms: Negative word-of-mouth dynamics in social media networks. *Journal of Marketing Communications, 20*(1–2), 117–128.

Schulenkorf, N., & Frawley, S. (2017). *Critical issues in global sport management*. London: Routledge.

Shamir, B., Dayan-Horesh, H., & Adler, D. (2005). Leading by biography: Towards a life-story approach to the study of leadership. *Leadership, 1*(1), 13–29.

Smith, S. (2018). "Transcript: The Smith and Bancroft ball-tampering confession", *Sydney Morning Herald*, 25 March 2018, viewed 20 April 2018, https://www.smh.com.au/sport/cricket/transcript-the-smith-and-bancroft-ball-tampering-confession-20180325-p4z65c.html

Stensholt, J. (2018). "Cricket Australia can't keep control over its players: Analysis", *Australian Financial Review*, 27 March 2018, viewed 10 May 2018, https://search-proquest-com.ezproxy.lib.uts.edu.au/docview/2017967797?rfr_id=info%3Axri%2Fsid%3Aprimo

Sunstein, C. (2001). "The daily we: Is the internet really a blessing for democracy?" *Boston Review*, 1 June 2001, viewed 15 May 2018, http://bostonreview.net/cass-sunstein-internet-democracy-daily-we

The Ethics Centre. (2018). *Australian cricket: A matter of balance*. Sydney: The Ethics Centre.

Tucker, S., Turner, N., Barling, J., Reid, E., & Elving, C. (2006). Apologies and transformational leadership. *Journal of Business Ethics, 63*, 195–207.

10 Global sport leadership
Critical issues and future research

In our introductory chapter we argued that sport is a business involving intense emotions and many complexities. Research on leadership in the sporting realm spans the spaces of professional sport leagues, mega-events, community sport clubs, and voluntary programmes delivering community-based sport in disadvantaged communities. With this, there needs to be a consideration of the types of leadership skills and behaviours needed to be successful in *each of these* sport environments. We argue that this means understanding issues of fairness, access, and opportunity alongside larger goals of economic, social, health, and environmental returns. In this book, we have addressed a range of sporting realms that bring to light various facets of how sport is developed and delivered. Leadership is relevant to all of these domains and, as we have described, there are numerous theoretical perspectives for considering sport leadership.

The aim of the book has been to engage sport management scholars and students with current, critical, and applied sport leadership approaches. In order to achieve this aim, we have explored key leadership issues facing sport managers ranging from issues of social identity, leadership development, the unique and changing demands of high performance sport environments, contextual and social challenges of leadership in sport for development (SFD) environments, and reconciling leadership failure. The critical approach that we have taken in this book has offered each of the scholars involved the opportunity to consider their own practical work and scholarly perspective in relation to leadership. To be fair, none of the scholars herein can claim to be experts in leadership in their own right, but each of us have diverse expertise on the topics and the realms of sport in which we have addressed critical leadership issues. As such, we hope to have offered a unique perspective that critically examines the dynamic nature of leadership in a variety of contexts from a critical management perspective. Given our underlying philosophies of research – united by the idea that sport has the potential to play a positive role in society when led appropriately – our aim has been to highlight leadership issues that move this agenda forward. We acknowledge the long history of corruption and ethical challenges in sport and thus hope that we have offered some new insights into sport leadership that are designed to foster a more just and equitable sport environment. Our varying perspectives have been an interesting source of discussion in terms of how the theoretical underpinnings of leadership from sociological, historical, psychological, and management perspectives coalesce in the sporting domain. In this final discussion, we offer some insights for the future of research and scholarship on leadership in sport that stem from the discussions presented in this book.

Approaching leadership research in sport

In the introductory chapter, we discussed three interconnected levels at which sport is led: meta, macro, and micro. For the most part, we have focussed on the macro level in this book, with some perspectives on the micro level. The 'meta' level of leadership is challenging for researchers to address because it describes the 'big picture' processes of people exerting influence through creating a 'global' vision that attracts engaged followers. We discuss this perspective in relation to mega-events and in high performance sport. Examples of leaders with a significant global visioning influence typically come from large sporting/political organisations. An example would be the vision of Juan Antonio Samaranch for the Olympic Games and the associated global movement. This meta perspective is about the powerful vision that drives a larger agenda around sport and is often disconnected from the everyday happenings of sport. Perhaps, given the significant issues of corruption and scandals that currently plague international sport, we should dedicate more time and attention to meta perspectives in future work. We hope that students and scholars will consider the meta perspective of leadership in sport and how it influences other areas of sport.

The space that has received the greatest amount of attention in this book has centred on the macro perspective of leadership. Macro perspectives concern the building of successful organisations and programmes. Many of the leadership theories employed in this book, such as the social identity approach, multiple linkage model, servant leadership, and shared leadership offer insights at the macro level of organisations. An interesting feature of each perspective is the primacy of sociocultural factors in explaining successful leadership, such as the context and the environment in which leaders act. In this sense, we examine leadership from a top-down perspective in that we address the behaviours, traits, and characteristics that leaders use to galvanise followers. Yet bottom-up perspectives are also important as leaders are more successful if they are able to exemplify characteristics that are valued by the groups they lead. Thus, we have shared the importance of understanding leadership as a dynamic construct in a number of applied settings.

To a lesser extent, we have also tried to address some of the micro level factors associated with leadership and success in sport organisations. For example, understanding individual-level character is an important micro context for considering the ways in which people can effectively lead organisations towards larger macro goals of social justice in sport. The important part of this discussion stems from some of the early concepts of leadership when traits alone were not enough to explain successful leaders. Rather, the situational context is highly relevant to the success of leaders, but also clearly related to the way in which individual leaders react and behave in the context of each situation. Again, we note the contextual and dynamic nature of leadership. This is highlighted in some detail throughout the book, and in particular, the #Sandpapergate case presented in Chapter 9. It offers the perspective of bringing together the micro level factors of the leader themselves with other influential levels of the organisational context and the greater vision for success in professional sport. The case highlights the need to consider the failures and successes in sport to determine how best to discuss successful leadership practices.

Theoretical insights

As described in the introductory chapter of the book, Goff (2005) has noted that great sporting leaders need to be intellectually astute, engaged in critical thinking, and creative above the bottom line expectations that can all too often creep into management. Considering this, it is essential to understand the types of mental strengths, character perspectives, relationships with members, and overall abilities in addressing the interpersonal and management challenges of sport organisations. We argue that non-sporting domains such as business, psychology, and sociology could learn a great deal from sport leadership – and vice versa. Yet the theoretical depth of sport leadership remains relatively shallow, often relying on traditional understandings of leadership. Certainly, while there is a lot of value in knowledge transfer across disciplinary boundaries, sport leadership remains a developing field of study that requires theoretical creativity and rigour to foster new investigations to further the field. With this book, we have offered some novel perspectives on considering leadership. In the following paragraphs, we outline some future agendas for research in relation to the areas of leadership discussed.

Social identity leadership

The social identity approach has been used in sport management scholarship to explore team identification (e.g. Lock & Heere, 2017; Lock, Taylor, Funk & Darcy, 2012), discrimination (Cunningham & Sagas, 2005), and diversity (Cunningham, 2005). Yet it has received much less attention in relation to leadership behaviours. We have argued that a social identity approach can offer a theoretically informed perspective that emphasises how leaders achieve power through groups rather than over groups. In this sense, leaders that are sensitive to what group members value in certain situations can galvanise individuals into an empowered collective seeking to deliver on organisational visions. This occurs when followers internalise the shared features of a group and leaders embody meaningful aspects of the group identity. Given the constantly fluctuating and evolving contexts of sport organisations, research needs to address how leaders can support the group identity needs of followers and devise strategies to bring members together around a shared vision in contexts that change quickly. Some of the recent research addressing this approach has been highlighted in Chapter 2 and offers a shift away from the ideal leader characteristics conveyed in older work towards understanding the contextual nature of sporting environments and the dynamics of leadership that make certain leadership characteristics prototypical and successful in the social context.

The social identity approach to leadership (Haslam, Reicher, & Platow, 2010; Hogg, 2001) provides a range of opportunities to develop, contrast, or challenge existing leadership theorising in sport. As we have shown, the theories that underpin research in different domains of sport vary quite significantly. As such, there are opportunities to consider the relevance of the social identity approach in, for example, SFD and diversity. In SFD, the social identity approach offers a potential extension to the servant and shared leadership perspectives we have discussed. Both are only possible in groups with clear understandings of what matters to group members.

In relation to the arguments about diversity, the social identity approach presents some pertinent opportunities. As we discussed, character is a crucial aspect of leadership in relation to diversity. However, the evaluation of, for example, character or charisma has been shown to vary based on the extent to which a leader embodies shared and meaningful features of a group (Platow et al., 2006). Furthermore, understanding the contextual features of a group provides an important insight into the 'characters' or characteristics that might be more successful. Given the importance of leader character to diversity research, therefore, developing knowledge about the role shared identity plays in evaluations of leaders' character offers a key point to advance knowledge.

Leadership development

Given the lack of research that has been conducted on leadership development in sporting contexts, the scope for future studies is wide and deep. Future research should start by comparing different cultural contexts and moving beyond North America and Europe to explore the different approaches to leadership development within sporting organisations and contexts in order to broaden the sport management knowledge base (Frawley, Favaloro, & Schulenkorf, 2018). A large limiting factor for leadership development for many sporting organisations is the lack of available resources that can be invested over time in relevant programmes and strategies. Future research should explore examples of best practice for leadership development in sport organisations with limited resources in order to develop knowledge on low-cost programmes and strategies that can be deployed by senior management and human resource departments. Finally, and most importantly, sport leadership development research needs to expand beyond professional sport organisations into more diverse community-based sport organisations. Through an examination of both large and small sport organisations we can develop a fuller picture of the leadership development environment and where the gaps are that need to be filled from both a research and practice perspective.

Cross-border leadership

In Chapter 5, we defined cross-border leadership as *an inclusive and dynamic process of listening, learning, challenging, influencing, guiding, and motivating others across diverse contexts and backgrounds with the intent of leading them towards a relevant, meaningful, and coherent goal.* We argue that this definition establishes an intriguing and rather 'open' space for further investigation, as it provides an inclusive framework for practical application. In this book, we have specifically discussed examples of sport leadership across geographical, sociocultural, generational, sporting, and/or organisational borders. In the future, researchers might look at leadership across (sport) political spheres or discuss structural elements of cross-border engagements. Also, an investigation into specific traits related to the different 'borders' could be conducted to highlight people's expectations and necessary characteristics or skills for future leaders. Such investigations could have immediate practical implications for sport organisations that aim to develop or recruit the most qualified cross-border leaders.

Successful cross-border leadership requires theoretically informed perspectives that disrupt the status quo thinking about sport and consideration for socially, culturally, and contextually relevant approaches. This is particularly important in SFD settings, where cross-border leadership is often necessary for delivering sport. Cross-border leadership offers a different theoretical approach for scholars as it identifies an inclusive and dynamic process of listening, learning, challenging, influencing, guiding, and motivating others across diverse contexts and backgrounds. The intention remains to lead teams and organisations towards a relevant, meaningful, and coherent set of goals that support innovative, inclusive sporting environments. However, the approach offers a new way of thinking about the role of leaders in relation to the participants involved in SFD programmes.

Sport mega-events

Leadership strategy related to sport mega-events has been a relatively understudied area. Yet the prevalence and complexity of mega-events would suggest that there is a need to consider further leadership practices and theoretical understandings within the events landscape. From the bid phase through to the event conclusion and legacy phase, there are many considerations regarding appropriate leadership skills, character, and contextual approaches. Certainly, leaders require highly developed political and media skills in the mega-events environment. As highlighted in the chapter on mega-events, the research of Parent and colleagues (2008, 2009) has pointed to models such as the multiple linkages approach to begin to consider the complexity of leadership throughout the life cycle of the event. Yet further theoretical approaches, such as leader character and high performance leadership, require consideration if events are to remain successful. The context of urban development remains another key consideration in how events are shaped and driven within the context of civic development strategies. Theoretical approaches from urban studies can offer some unique advances to understanding leadership perspectives in the interplay between the event and the civic development agenda. The works of Mason, Sant, and Misener (2018) and Misener and Mason (2008, 2009) offer starting points to introduce urban development approaches to leadership in sport mega-events.

Given the challenges faced by international sport organisations in the mega-events space, such as cities dropping out of races to host the Olympic and Paralympic Games, there is increasing pressure on leaders to work with multiple partners from government, public, and private sectors, and to operate as a conduit to the media. Events might also require different types of leadership at different phases of the events processes, and thus future research can examine and consider the shifting roles, responsibilities, and opportunities for leaders in each of these phases. From the planning phase, where there are significant managerial functions that a leader needs to be involved with to the all-important legacy processes which require approaches such as servant leadership to ensure community stakeholders are considered. There is not one model of leadership that fits well in the mega-events process, but research in the future should consider how different approaches and strategies influence the outcome of an event. Each event is unique and thus leadership research needs to address the distinctive needs and desires of the particular sport mega-event in relation to the social and cultural context in which it takes place.

Diversity leadership

Despite an emphasis in the sport literature on the challenges of the lack of diversity in many sport settings, there is scant literature that addresses how to foster and engage leadership that enhances diversity and inclusion. The concerns about leader diversity remain problematic where research clearly points to inequity in representation of women and other minority groups. While scholars have voiced these concerns in the literature, the structure of sport can often perpetuate inequitable representations through leadership that promotes and advances the status quo. We have argued that two potential approaches – servant leadership and leader character – might offer the disruptive potential needed to reconsider equity and inclusion in sport leadership. Yet there need to be other considerations and approaches to how leaders can foster more diverse and inclusive environments. Most models of leadership have emerged from research that privileges a white male perspective. Therefore, such approaches offer little understanding of other perspectives that would support sporting efforts for more diverse leadership. Further, it remains clear that reward systems, hiring practices, and ultimately the culture of sport will need to shift if we expect to have more leaders that support inclusive practices. This remains a significant gap in the sport and leadership literature requiring innovative ideas and attention to the power relations in how sport and leadership are structured.

Sport for development

Our brief review of servant leadership and shared leadership in the context of SFD has identified a number of challenges for SFD organisations and their part- ners, as well as related opportunities for future SFD practice and research. First, in this global era, the cross-cultural aspects of servant leadership deserve more attention. Van Dierendonck (2011) has previously suggested that an important focus for future research is to investigate whether servant leadership is more likely to occur in countries with a strong humane orientation and a lower power- distance index (macro level), or if experiences are indeed more specifically related to individuals and their leadership style (micro level). Furthermore, the extent to which servant leadership is experienced differently across national contexts and within multinational settings deserves to be explored. As discussed, in an SFD setting – where cross-cultural engagement between stakeholders is common and certainly not without controversy – empirical studies on the characteristics of local and international servant leaders are welcome. Adding to those studies could be research that engages in comparative multi-case studies that investigate the strategies and processes employed by different SFD leaders with the intent of contributing to SFD-specific theoretical frameworks and/or recommendations for best practice around leadership.

In advancing SFD-specific leadership studies, something can be learned from the area of youth sport development where examinations of creating, managing, and leveraging leadership have already been conducted (e.g. Gould & Voelker, 2010; Martinek, Schilling, & Hellison, 2006; Vella, Oades, & Crowe, 2013). In particular, Gould and Voelker (2010) discussed efforts to develop leadership through an educational approach to the sport captaincy experience. In their study they highlighted that sport coaches can play numerous important roles in the process – including that of mentors, teachers, and critical supporters. It seems that sport managers can learn from these experiences; in fact, by adding empirical socio-managerial research, SFD scholars may be able to contribute to the development of strong, inclusive, and well-respected SFD leaders under different leadership types.

High performance leadership

In relation to high performance leadership, there are two fascinating areas for future development. First, we discussed how existing work brings together lead- ers of sport at a variety of 'high performing' levels. Athlete-based research has spent considerable time isolating the qualities of super-elite performers (Hardy et al., 2017; Rees et al., 2016) in contrast to other levels of athlete (i.e. Team GB squad members), university, sport, etc. This work now presents a picture that super-elite athletes have some unique characteristics (e.g. are more likely to have experienced serious trauma at some point) than non-medalling athletes. It would be useful to observe whether leaders of super-elite athletes also display certain characteristics. To offer a broad and inclusive review of present knowledge on high performance leadership, we included work that involved leading an array of levels and some roles (national performance directors) that oversaw athletes from talent identification through to medal-winning performance. However, further knowledge of the characteristics that equip some individuals (if any) to lead at the highest levels of sport would extend present knowledge considerably.

Second, the high performance leadership literature has focussed on national performance directors, coaches, and athletes. Yet we know less about figures that occupy higher levels of management in sport (e.g. CEOs of National Governing Bodies). As key shapers of vision, funding allocation, and liaisons with other organisations, the upper management of national governing bodies would present a fascinating group to study in the future. In terms of creating strong visions that lead to sustained performance success at the elite level, research of this nature seems critical.

Failed leadership

In the chapter on failed leadership, we analysed the #Sandpapergate case. During this case, the Australian Cricket team and Cricket Australia displayed a range of leadership failures and deficiencies that offer fruitful grounds for future analysis. Of more relevance to future research are the relationship between leadership, the media (and social media), and crisis. As our analysis demonstrates, #Sandpapergate unfolded in layers and, over time, created new and different challenges for leaders of the team (i.e. Smith and Lehmann) and leaders of Cricket Australia (i.e. James Sutherland). Because of the way in which the scrutiny of leadership failures spreads through the media and social media, organisations need to be led ably at all times but proactively and authentically during crises. The online firestorms that emerged at different points in this case highlight that failed leadership does not lead to uniform or static responses from key audiences. Rather, as new information is revealed (e.g. Warner's role in the case), new challenges emerge for leaders that require Herculean efforts if the ship is to be steadied.

Conclusion

In essence, part of what we have tried to propose is a set of theoretically grounded understandings of leadership in sport with the intertwining of foundational concepts such as leadership development. What we also aimed to consider was how to disrupt traditional leadership perspectives that have shaped the ways in which we think about sport. We aimed to consider leadership as a way to develop a more socially just sport system. To this end, we have advanced arguments for the consideration of contextually appropriate and sensitive theoretical perspectives. In the chapter on diversity, we emphasised the breadth of research on diversity issues in sport, but the lack of empirically based research on advancing diversity and inclusion. While examples such as experience-based leadership by McCall (2010) are useful frameworks for professional sport organisations to maximise leadership and management potential, such normative theoretical approaches might not be as appropriate for diverse contexts such as SFD agendas. As we noted in Chapter 1, sport has been considered an important milieu for management research (Wolfe et al., 2005) and yet leadership studies in and through sport have continued to be relatively scarce (Fletcher & Wagstaff, 2009). Thus, we challenge students and scholars alike to think in new and different ways about leadership in sport that will contribute to bringing the theoretical approaches and practical implications closer together. Through these new perspectives and approaches, we can offer innovative perspectives on critical areas of global sport leadership.

References

Cunningham, G. B. (2005). The importance of a common in-group identity in ethnically diverse groups. *Group Dynamics: Theory, Research, and Practice, 9*(4), 251.

Cunningham, G. B., & Sagas, M. (2005). Access discrimination in intercollegiate athletics. *Journal of Sport and Social Issues, 29*(2), 148–163.

Fletcher, D., & Wagstaff, C. R. (2009). Organizational psychology in elite sport: Its emergence, application and future. *Psychology of Sport and Exercise, 10*(4), 427–434.

Frawley, S., Favaloro, D., & Schulenkorf, N. (2018). Experience-based leadership development and professional sport organizations. *Journal of Sport Management, 32*(2), 123–134.

Goff, B. L. (2005). *From the ballfield to the boardroom: Management lessons from sports.* Westport, CT: Greenwood Publishing Group.

Gould, D., & Voelker, D. K. (2010). Youth sport leadership development: Leveraging the sports captaincy experience. *Journal of Sport Psychology in Action, 1*(1), 1–14.

Hardy, L., Barlow, M., Evans, L., Rees, T., Woodman, T., & Warr, C. (2017). Great British medalists: Response to the commentaries. *Progress in Brain Research, 232,* 207–216.

Haslam, S. A., Reicher, S. D., & Platow, M. J. (2010). *The new psychology of leadership: Identity, influence and power.* London: Psychology Press.

Hogg, M. A. (2001). A social identity theory of leadership. *Personality and Social Psychology Review, 5*(3), 184–200.

Lock, D., & Heere, B. (2017). Identity crisis: A theoretical analysis of 'team identification' research. *European Sport Management Quarterly, 17,* 413–435.

Lock, D., Taylor, T., Funk, D., & Darcy, S. (2012). Exploring the development of team identification. *Journal of Sport Management, 26*(4), 283–294.

Martinek, T., Schilling, T., & Hellison, D. (2006). The development of compassionate and caring leadership among adolescents. *Physical Education and Sport Pedagogy, 11*(2), 141–157.

Mason, D., Sant, S. L., & Misener, L. (2018). Leveraging sport and entertainment facilities in small- to mid-sized cities. *Marketing Intelligence & Planning, 36*(2), 154–167.

McCall, M. W. (2010). Recasting leadership development. *Industrial Organisational Psychology, 3*(1), 3–19.

Misener, L., & Mason, D. S. (2008). Urban regimes and the sporting events agenda: A cross-national comparison of civic development strategies. *Journal of Sport Management, 22*(5), 603–627.

Misener, L., & Mason, D. S. (2009). Fostering community development through sporting events strategies: An examination of urban regime perceptions. *Journal of Sport Management, 23*(6), 770–794.

Parent, M. M., & Séguin, B. (2008). Toward a model of brand creation for international large-scale sporting events: The impact of leadership, context, and nature of the event. *Journal of Sport Management, 22*(5), 526–549.

Parent, M. M., Olver, D., & Séguin, B. (2009). Understanding leadership in major sporting events: The case of the 2005 World Aquatics Championships. *Sport Management Review, 12*(3), 167–184.

Platow, M. J., van Knippenberg, D., Haslam, S. A., van Knippenberg, B., & Spears, R. (2006). A special gift we bestow on you for being representative of us: Considering leader charisma from a self-categorization perspective. *British Journal of Social Psychology, 45*(2), 303–320.

Rees, T., Hardy, L., Güllich, A., Abernethy, B., Côté, J., Woodman, T., … Warr, C. (2016). The great British medalists project: A review of current knowledge on the development of the world's best sporting talent. *Sports Medicine, 46*(8), 1041–1058.

Wolfe, R. A., Weick, K. E., Usher, J. M., Terborg, J. R., Poppo, L., Murrell, A. J., … Jourdan, J. S. (2005). Sport and organizational studies: Exploring synergy. *Journal of Management Inquiry, 14*(2), 182–210.

Van Dierendonck, D. (2011). Servant leadership: A review and synthesis. *Journal of Management, 37*(4), 1228–1261.

Vella, S. A., Oades, L. G., & Crowe, T. P. (2013). The relationship between coach leadership, the coach–athlete relationship, team success, and the positive developmental experiences of adolescent soccer players. *Physical Education and Sport Pedagogy, 18*(5), 549–561.

Index

CPSIA information can be obtained
at www.ICGtesting.com
Printed in the USA
BVHW050104210223
658858BV00017B/321

9 780367 671273